LESSONS LEARNED FROM DATING

MOVING PAST
THE HURT INTO YOUR BLESSINGS

KARLA L. MCCULLUM

LESSONS LEARNED FROM DATING

MOVING PAST THE HURT INTO YOUR BLESSINGS

I dedicate this book to my beautiful daughter, K. K, continue to always put God first in your life, work hard and accomplish all of your dreams. You are beautiful, intelligent, kind, loving, and blessed. I am beyond blessed to have you as my daughter.

TABLE OF CONTENTS

PREFACE

"So do not fear, for I am with you; do not be dismayed, for I am your God." - Isaiah 41:10, NIV

Dating for me has been a challenge. I have dated different types of men: thugs, geeks, lovers, fighters, you name it. Each beau came with his own unique experience, and I learned something new from each one of them. We shared lots of laughs and good times, but I always ended with the same result, a broken heart. In most cases, I held on longer than I should have, just to have a man in my life. Even when it was clear I needed to run, not walk, away, I would not.

Thankfully, maturity comes with age, and as I got older, I would not hold on as long, but I still stayed around longer than I should have. One day I realized something just was not right, but I did not know what. I asked myself why I ended up with the same results every time I dated. I finally concluded I had to do something different to get a different result, so I started working on the one person I had control over, and that was me. Consequently, I started to do the self-work and began healing with the goal of being a healed woman of God. I wrote this book as the last part of my healing journey, but more importantly, I am also sharing my story with the hope of helping other women. I want to encourage women to permanently escape the toxic dating cycle, find their peace, and discover who God wants them to be. You are not alone. Other women have fallen for the counterfeits and misfits and had a good man that broke their hearts.

My prayer is that this book will help start the healing process, not just of toxic relationships, but your entire mind, body, and soul. Look to God and be encouraged.

ACKNOWLEDGMENTS

First, I want to give honor to God, who is the head of my life. I thank Him for giving me the vision to write this book. For always providing and covering me and for never leaving me. Thank you, Father God, for all past, present, and future.

Secondly, I want to acknowledge my alpha and beta readers. Renee, I am thankful to you for taking the time to be my first editor and reviewing, providing comments, and giving honest feedback from the very first rough draft until I turned the book in for publishing. I believe you, and I went through four edits and reviews of this book. I chose you as my alpha reader not only because of your outstanding editing skills but also because you know me so well. We have thirty-plus years of friendship, and I am grateful to have you as a friend, more like a sister. Thank you!

Next, I want to thank my beta readers. Carrie and Yevette, you two are awesome! You read my book and provided great feedback and edits as well. You ladies rock! I appreciate both of you for the time, dedication, and hard work in helping me accomplish this mission.

I cannot forget about my family! To my mother, father, grandmothers, siblings, aunts, uncles, and all my family, thank you for praying, encouraging, and believing in me. I love you all.

"I will instruct you and teach you in the way you should go;" I will counsel you with my loving eye on you" - *Psalms 32:8, NIV*

BACK IN THE DAY

"Your past was meant to be school, not jail." - Lalah Lovebliss

Growing up in the late 80s and early 90s was the absolute best! We did not realize it at the time, but we had so much fun! One of the activities we looked forward to was playing outside. Once we were outside, my girlfriends and I would meet up to play hand games like Rockin' Robin, Slide Baby, and one of my favorites, Uno, dos-ee-ay-say. We also played other games like Hopscotch and Jacks. I loved playing jacks; I could not quite get past the two's, but it was all fun.

Bike riding was also a favorite in my neighborhood. We would race each other on our bikes or roller-skate up and down our block. It was all so awesome. When the boys were around, we would play Hide and Seek or Tag with them. For the most part, the girls played with the girls, and the boys played with the boys. The boys were rough, but I was somewhat rough too, and I have the scars on my legs to prove it. I have fallen, skinned my knees, and bruised my elbows and other parts of my body from jumping off the swing, running too hard or just playing around outside. I never broke any bones, thank God. The worst I had was a badly sprained ankle I received after falling while roller-skating down the sidewalk in front of my house.

I remember getting excited when I heard the ice cream man coming. I would run in the house to get a dollar from my mother so that I could get a bomb pop or an ice cream sandwich, or on Tuesdays when the candy bus would come around my way, I would run home from school so I could get my sunflower seeds and "nowlaters" (Now & Later candy).

When I was younger, we did not have cell phones. There was only a house phone, and if someone called your parents on the other line, you had to end your call. Like most little girls and teenagers, I loved talking on the phone. To avoid having the house phone ring late at night, I would call the number that told us the time (yes, we were able to call a number to get the exact time), so my other line would beep instead of the phone ringing. That way, the ringing phone would not wake my parents up. If my parents knew I was up that late on the phone, I would have been punished.

When I was in the eighth grade, my parents got me a pager. You could not tell me anything with my pager. We had special codes, and if someone wanted to talk late at night, all they had to do is page me, and I would call them back. Today kids will never know about the not-so-techy days, but we were creative and had a fun time with it. Life was so fun and free then.

Summertime was the best as a child. During the summer months, one of my closest friends, Rhonda, and I would attend summer camp at a local church. We had a blast! The camp was about two months long and ran from 8 am to 4 pm from Monday to Friday. Each day, the camp counselors had a different fun activity planned, but you could not participate in the activities if you had discipline issues. I had discipline issues, but I did not during camp because I did not want to miss any of the festivities. Wednesdays were swim days. All approved to go swimming would get changed into their swimsuits at the church and board the bus to be taken to a local swimming pool for fun.

The summer before I went to the fifth grade, I attended this camp, and I was so excited about going swimming because my mother had bought me the cutest two-piece swimsuit. It was a neon green bandeau top with a multicolored neon ruffle skirt bottom. I could not wait to show it off, especially to the cutie in my summer camp class. His name was Lester, and I thought he was so cute.

On the first day of swimming at the camp, I hurried into the bathroom, changed into my new two-piece swimsuit, and hurried back into class to make sure I was sitting right next to the cutie Lester. Once inside the classroom and sitting next to Lester, I started smiling and flirting, or whatever you want to call it, at that age. Lester was not paying me any attention. He was trying to talk to his boys that were also sitting at the table.

I remember I tapped him on the shoulder to get his attention when Rhonda interrupted the class with an announcement that someone had dropped their panties in the hallway. No one claimed them, and I did not even look because I was focused on Lester. Then Rhonda said, "Wait, Karla, are these your panties?" I looked, and sure enough, they were mine. After I changed, I was moving so fast that I did not realize I dropped my panties in the hallway outside of my locker. As the class laughed, I was so embarrassed, but I had to play it off and be cool about it. I believe this was the beginning of my boy crazy years.

Once middle school started, and I grew into my teenage years, I became even crazier about boys, and once my parents transferred me to a private catholic school for my seventh-grade year, I believe my boy craze became ten times worse. Rhonda had attended the school I was transferred to for most of her academic career. I was happy she was there because I knew I had at least one friend at the school. The class size was small, and within a matter of weeks, I made more friends.

One girl in the class and I hit it off well, and we grew to become quite close. We were BFFs before BFFs were a thing. Her name was China. She was an only child and extremely spoiled. Hanging with China was cool because her mother was not as strict as mine. So, whenever we hooked up, it was usually at her house or leaving her house to go out. Whenever we were together, it was always a good time. Now, I was boy crazy, but she was at a higher level of craziness, and together we were the ultimate boy crazy.

My friend Rhonda was mainly focused on her academic career. She found an after-school program at a local private all-boys catholic high school that helped with the higher levels of algebra. Once China and I found out about this class and where it was being held, we were sold on taking the class, and no, we did not take it to learn algebra. Did I mention the class was being held at an all-boys private high school, and we liked older boys? China and I went to see what we could catch while there.

I told my parents about the class, and they thought it was a good idea to attend, but I never told them there was a cost and never paid for it. I knew my parents would have told me no because they were already paying my tuition for regular school. No extra funds were coming out of the house, but that would not stop me from flirting with these high school boys.

I am not sure why, but the teacher allowed us to attend free for a while. He eventually told China and me not to return because we were late and disrupting the class. We, however, did not tell our parents that we were not allowed to go to class or we needed funding for class. Instead, we continued to show up to the school as if we were taking the class because, at this point, we found some cute sophomores to flirt with, so we did have a reason for going to the school. I believe we told the boys we were eighth graders instead of seventh graders to be a little closer to them in age. All the while, Rhonda was attending the math class preparing herself for high school.

During the summers while in middle school, Rhonda, who lived five doors up from me, and I would sit on the front porch (hers or mine) and gossip like two old ladies. We both had a crush on the older guy who lived in the halfway house between ours. His name was Roman. Roman was four or five years older than us, tall and absolutely handsome. We would sit on the porch and wait for him to come outside so we could stare at him. We would argue over who he liked when he did not want either one of us in reality. I would fantasize about marrying Roman. I just knew he would be my husband in the future, but until then, there were other boys for me to flirt with and make my "boyfriend."

The older I got, the more my boy craziness grew into an unhealthy obsession with men. I would fall in love with potential and work hard to try to change or sculpt the man to be who I wanted him to be. I would give so much of myself to him so he would love me back. I went through a phase where I did not want to be single, so whoever I was with, I would stay with just because I did not want to be alone. No matter how bad he treated me or how much he lied to me, I would not leave.

I used to look at being single as a curse and thought I needed to be in a relationship. That was a requirement in life. It was not until I took a break from dating I realized being single is a real blessing. Being single helped me to learn to love myself. It was time for me to get closer to God and grow as a woman.

Through it all, God has covered me and blessed me. I was never physically abused, but I have been mentally and emotionally abused, lied to, cheated on, and had other traumatizing experiences. Reflecting on past relationships and men I have dated, I realized there were lessons and blessings in it all. A few lessons were not learned the first time around and had to be repeated a few times. All were significant experiences I needed to assist me in growing into the woman I am today. Those lessons were used to prepare me to walk in my purpose and to prepare me for my purpose partner. I now view my real life lessons as blessings that have led me to discover and love the real me.

HIGH SCHOOL

"For I know the plans I have for you" declares the Lord, "plans to prosper you and not to harm you, plans to give you hope and a future." - Jeremiah 29:11, NIV

I dated a few characters in high school, a few nice guys, and a few buttholes. Overall, I did not have that bad of a dating experience. True, I was young and did not know what I wanted in a "boyfriend," and technically, according to my mom, I was not even supposed to be dating, but I dated, or at least what I thought was dating.

I was able to talk on the phone to boys, and that is what my dating life consisted of. Occasionally we would meet up downtown after school and get something to eat, or the gentleman I was dating at the time would just walk me to the bus stop because I had to be home by a certain time. Most of the beaus I met through a friend or downtown when I was hanging with my friends after school. I went to an all-girls school, so I could not meet boys in school, but I always found a way to meet them.

The first guy I dated was Nathan. We were secretly dating because, as I said, I was not allowed to have a boyfriend. We did not do much but talk on the phone. He was not a nice guy. He was definitely a butthole. There was something smooth about him, and he had a car! I was a freshman, and he was a junior in high school. My friend China introduced us. She was dating his best friend, Earl. I do not remember how China and Earl met, but about a month or two after they started dating, she hooked me up with Nathan.

He was tall, had an athletic build and he was somewhat cute. He was a few years older than I was, but that was cool. I always liked dating older men. Nathan would lie so smoothly you did not even realize what was going on. I would smile and shake my head in agreement because I was so into him. I was gullible.

It was not until months after we stopped talking that I found out he was a liar. I was young and naïve, so I believed everything that he told me. I trusted him, and when I caught him talking to another girl, and he said she was just a friend, that meant she was just a friend. I believed him when he said I was special. We would go days or even weeks without talking or seeing one another. Whatever excuse or lie that Nathan gave me when he finally called, I fell for it and was back to being his girl.

I was immature and had a lot to learn, and he was only the first of a few deceivers. The final straw that ended it with Nathan was when he called me on three-way with another girl. The girl asked me when the last time he and I talked was. It had been a few weeks, and I told her that, but I went to explain more about how I was his girl, and I did not get to finish because he hung up on me. I was done. He had the audacity to call me a week later and acted as if nothing happened. He really played like what happened a few weeks ago did not happen. I laughed and hung up. It was over. The smooth lies did not work anymore.

About a year later, I met Felix. He was older, tall, and slim, and had a lighter complexion. We met on the number 20 bus after school. That day my friends and I caught the light rail from school to downtown Baltimore to take pictures at Moe's. My friends and I would do that often after school. We would get the six for $6 photo special; sometimes pay a little extra for a double exposure photo because they were the best. Once we were done, we would grab some food and then head home.

On this day, after we were done eating and flicking it up at the photo studio, I hopped on the number 20 bus to head home. Felix got on the stop after me, sat next to me and he started talking to me. Before I got off the bus, he asked for my number, and I gave it to him. He called me that night, and we stayed on the phone for hours. Before I knew it, we started our crazy relationship.

Felix was 19 years old and out of school, but he did not graduate or have a GED. His occupation was a street pharmacist, and he lived with his mom. About six months into our relationship, Felix was arrested and ended up on house arrest.

Felix being on house arrest did not stop our relationship. He was cute and still was making money. I did not ask questions, and he did not offer any answers. I would cut school or lie about going out with a girlfriend so I could go over to his mom's house and visit him. We continued to date for a little while, but I got tired of it. We could not go anywhere, and I always had to go over to his mom's house, which was on the other side of town, to see him.

I was bored with the relationship, so I moved on, but I did not tell him. I would talk on the phone with him, but I always had a reason not to visit him. I had a new friend I liked to spend time with, and I did not tell Felix. He was on house arrest. What could he do? So I would go out with my friend and have a good time.

I also talked to other guys. I even went on a date or two with them. Once I realized he was getting impatient and could tell something had changed, I told him I did not want this relationship anymore. Of course, he did not make it easy to walk away. He would call and threaten to hurt me. "How?" I would ask. "You cannot leave the house." It was a joke to me. Now that I am older, I realize it was not a joke. A man threatening to hurt you is no laughing matter. He ended up doing something that landed him in jail and off house arrest. That was the end of Felix, at least that is what I thought.

Felix would call me collect from jail. I did not accept the charges. One, because I did not want to talk to him, and two, there was no way I was going to accept collect charges on my mama's phone. Me ignoring him while he was locked up did not stop him. Felix was persistent.

My mom and I had moved before he was released from prison, which at first I was upset about, but when he could not find me, I saw how much of a blessing that move was. My mom had her number transferred to our new house, so he was still able to get in contact with me via phone. When he called, I would hang up.

In the beginning, when he was first released, he would call me daily. I was over him and did not want anything to do with him. Then he started calling less and less. After a few months of me hanging up on him, he finally left me alone. I never heard from him again. Hallelujah, it was finally over! No more Felix.

A few years went by, and I was single. After Felix, I needed a break. I dated a few guys, and at this point, I was able to go out on actual dates, but I was never in what I considered a relationship with them. We were just having fun, nothing serious.

During my senior year, I started dating my friend's brother. His name was Harry. I never looked at Harry as a boyfriend before; he was always my friend's older brother, nothing more. But something changed one night when I went to visit my friend.

I visited my friend at her sister's house to catch up, and her brother and his friend were there. We were all talking and having a good time. Harry's friend and my friend went into the other room to talk, and Harry and I stayed in the living room and talked. I was actually waiting for my date to pick me up and take me out. Our conversation was great! This was the first time I looked at him differently. He was handsome, intelligent, and funny.

Before I walked out the door for my date, Harry asked for my number and said he wanted to call me to make sure that I arrived home safely.

Just because I was allowed to date didn't mean I didn't have a curfew, and you better believe I was home that night by curfew. I didn't want any problems with my mother. About 10 minutes after I got home, Harry called me to make sure I was home. He and I talked until late in the night.

Harry was a year older and very independent. He was not as tall as previous suitors were, but taller than I, and a very slim man. I stopped talking to the man that took me out on a date that night, and all of my attention went to Harry. We dated most of my senior year of high school. He was the first man I brought home to meet my family. He spent Thanksgiving with me and my family, and he took me to meet his family for a family member's birthday celebration. My mom adored Harry. He was so respectful, and he was different from other men I had dated. Harry was my first love.

As I got closer to graduation, things were not going great between the two of us. We had planned for him to be my date for senior prom, but something was not right between us, and neither of us knew what it was. We did not talk as much, and when we were on the phone together, not much talking happened.

Right before my senior prom, we had a huge argument. I wanted him to wear a tuxedo, and he wanted to wear an expensive shirt he bought with some slacks. He told me he was wearing the shirt, and that was it. I told him exactly what he could do with his shirt and hung up the phone on him. After that, neither one of us tried to reach out to the other. We were over, just like that.

I could not believe it. I was heartbroken because I loved Harry. I ended up going to prom alone and lonely. That is when I started believing I did not need a man for anything; I felt like I could do it all by myself. This was my first real heartbreak, and I never took time to sit in my pain and heal. I did not know I needed to heal, and I did not know how to heal at the time.

The night of my graduation, my phone rang, and it was Harry. I was ecstatic to hear from him. He congratulated me on graduating from high school, and by the end of the call, we were back in a relationship, but it was not the same. I had a wall up, and I would not let down. My heart was guarded, and I did not trust him. I was scared of getting hurt. I just wanted to get away from him. I wanted away from Baltimore. I was angry because my heart was still broken, and I did not trust him. I also felt out of place at home and did not know what to do with my life.

I graduated from high school. Now what? I worked two part-time jobs and went to community college full time. I majored in computer programing but hated it. I was lost and had no idea what I wanted to do with my life. My co-worker at one of my part-time jobs suggested I join the army with her. At first, I was like, "Me? Join the army? Ha! I don't think so," but after a while, the idea grew on me and the February after I graduated high school, I enlisted in the United States Army. I didn't tell anyone until after I enlisted, not even Harry.

When I told him I enlisted, I was so nonchalant about it. He called me that night and asked me how my day was. I told him it was nice.

"I enlisted in the army, and I leave on March 30th."

Harry was silent, and then he said he had to go. The next day he called me to make sure he heard me correctly the day before. He asked if I enlisted and would be leaving in a month? After the initial shock wore off, Harry and I talked and decided to let our relationship go and remain friends. I put in my notice at my jobs and enjoyed my last few weeks of freedom before leaving for Basic Combat Training.

LESSONS

Most of the lessons I encountered while in high school were bilateral. One side was for me to know what to look for and what not to accept in my relationships. The other side was for me to evaluate myself as a woman of Christ and fix my negative traits, to be what I wanted to attract.

Respect, trust and honesty are the three top lessons taught during my high school years, and these three were definitely bilateral schoolings. Looking back at the relationships during that time, I was not being respectful, trusting, or honest in a few situations, but I wanted it in return. On a few occasions, I did not get it in return. I was being disrespectful in my relationship by not acknowledging the other person and just doing what I wanted to do. I was also disrespected by being ignored, cheated on, and lied to. Being dishonest breaks the trust in the relationship and is disrespectful to the other person.

Artist Lauryn Hill has a song called Ex-Factor from her debut solo album, The Miseducation of Lauryn Hill. I love the song and even at the young age of eighteen, that song hit home for me in so many different ways. One of the lines is, "Tell me who I have to be to get some reciprocity." Reciprocity was something that was not going on in the first relationship. I was there wholeheartedly, and he was there when he wanted to be, and for a while, that was ok with me because I did not know any better. I was ok with receiving nothing in return, but eventually, that got old, and I realized I deserved better.

This was only the first time the lesson, of giving the man all the power and allowing them to come and go freely in my life, or only giving of themselves when they felt like it, would appear in my dating life. Each time this lesson came, it was taught differently, but the last time the teacher taught it to me in a way that made me finally open my eyes and learn from it.

These three dating lessons left me broken-hearted and guarded. Not knowing at that time, I was young and naïve, and this was just the beginning of the lessons set for me to be taught. I never took time to heal or reflect on my past relationships so I would not repeat the same mistakes, so I did just that. I repeated some lessons several times until they were learned.

ARMY DAYS

"But as for you, be strong and do not give up for your work will be rewarded." - II Chronicles 15:7, NIV

In March 2000, I arrived at basic combat training (BCT) to start my new life as a soldier. Many believed I could not do it. I honestly did not believe I could do it, but with a lot of prayers and hard work, I graduated from BCT. After being held back in BCT for several weeks because I could not qualify with my weapon, I finally qualified, and in July 2000, I was finally released to start Advanced Individual Training (AIT). I arrived almost a month late, so I had to go through training with the class that was starting at the time of my arrival.

My co-worker, now battle buddy, that I joined the army with had finished BCT on time and was almost done with AIT when I arrived. Her class was like the seniors of AIT since they were next to graduate. She showed me the ropes my first couple of days there of what we could and could not do. She let me know which drill sergeants were not as strict as others were. We had a little more freedom once we made it to AIT, but it was still a strict environment.

After a few days, the next AIT class was starting, and I was in that training class. On the first day of training, I laid eyes on him. His name was Ernest. I do not know what it was about him, but he was beautiful, chocolate, had a nice build, not too tall, and had a great smile, and he was about five years older than I was. I thought to myself, oh, he is going to be mine.

I was in AIT, and my focus should have been on completing training and getting to my permanent duty station, but now it was on a man, and he is what I found more interesting. About a month into training, I could see that he was taking a liking to me. We would spend time together in the recreation room talking and laughing. He made me laugh until my stomach would hurt. I love to laugh, and he was very comical.

Training was eight weeks long, and for the first few weeks, we had on-post passes, where we would go anywhere on post. We would go to the bowling alley and bowl or grab some food from Burger King and bring it back to the barracks and eat in the recreation room. At the halfway point of training, soldiers who were doing well in classes, passed their PT test, and did not have any discipline issues would usually get to leave around noon and had to be back around 8 pm.

The first weekend we were granted an off-post pass, Ernest went off the post and returned drunk. I did not use my pass, so I was in my barracks room listening to music relaxing. It was our free time, and I decided to enjoy it. Suddenly one of my battle buddies (a fellow soldier in training with me) came running frantically into my barracks room. She said, "You better come get your boy. He is about to get in trouble."

She was referring to Ernest. I got up and went downstairs to the recreation room to see what was going on. When I arrived, I saw that Ernest was drunk, angry and about to fight two male soldiers!

I went over to where he was standing and started talking calmly to Ernest. I told him he needed to calm down before the drill sergeant came in there, and he got in trouble. After talking to him for a few minutes, he finally calmed down. That was my first time seeing that side of Ernest, and I did not like it. I was used to him being the funny, silly guy. Who was this drunk, angry man?

The next day when we finally saw each other, he apologized. He told me he didn't know what came over him the night before and promised that he wouldn't get like that anymore. We talked for a little while longer that day, and eventually, he went back to being that silly and fun guy I liked.

A few weekends went past. During that time, we would go off post together, go to the malls, and have fun and return. There were no issues, but one weekend he went with his friends, and I went with mine. When I returned to the barracks, Ernest was there already drunk and angry.

When I saw him, I thought, he does not need to drink if it brings this person out of him. He was drunk, angry, and ready to fight any man that stepped to him. I did not jump in this time to help ease the problem. I walked away and went to my room. I do not know what happened once I went upstairs, and I did not ask. He did not get into any trouble, so I assumed one of his friends helped him out.

The way Ernest acted when he was drunk was so unattractive. I stopped talking to him until the end of training.

On the day of our graduation, Ernest approached me and said, "You really are going to leave and not give me a hug."

"Of course not," I said as I hugged him. I thought this was the last time we would see each other.

"Can we keep in touch? I will be stationed in Alaska, but when I come home to Georgia to visit my family, I would love to see you. Do you think that would be okay?"

"Sure."

I gave him my mom's number and told him he can always find me through my mother as she has had the same number forever, and we parted ways.

A few months after I arrived at my duty station, I received a phone call one night, and it was Ernest. He called my mother, and she gave him my number in Georgia. It was so good hearing from him; I honestly missed him. We talked and laughed, and he told me he was coming home to visit family and wanted to know if he could come see me while in town. "Of course," I said.

A few weeks later, Ernest called me to let me know he arrived in Georgia and wanted to see me that weekend. I had butterflies in my stomach. The weekend could not get here fast enough. I was floating around the office smiling that Friday because I knew I would see Ernest that night, and I did.

He arrived on post Friday night, took me out to dinner, and stayed with me the entire weekend. That weekend we talked and laughed. We were free and really enjoyed ourselves. I felt so comfortable with him. I could talk to him about any and everything.

Once Monday came, he dropped me off at work (he did not get up with me at 530am for physical training (PT)) and took me to lunch that day. We had a great time! He told me that I was his one and only girl and that I was special, and he loved me. It was so sweet. I was so sad to see him leave Monday evening.

Once Ernest got back to Alaska, he called me and said, "Look, you are my girl," but we had developed a special bond with a unique understanding. Yes, I was his lady and he was my man, but we both knew we were stationed far away from each other. We both were trying to get to the same duty station, and we agreed that once we were stationed together, we would be an official couple, which I thought would be soon.

Ernest led me to believe that he put in a request for a change of duty station. He told me that he agreed to move so he could be closer to me and his family, and I believed him. I was elated, and I could not wait until we were together.

I agreed to Ernest's terms and accepted our unique relationship. Whenever he came home to visit his family, which was not very often, he would visit me too. I was ok with the sporadic visits. I understood the flight was expensive, and we did not make much as privates in the army. It also made sense for him to spend the money to come to Georgia so he could see his family and me, and when I was younger, I was scared of such a long flight, so I had no desire to fly to Alaska, but I am over that fear now.

While Ernest was living in Alaska, I started dating a man named Sherman. Sherman was a sergeant in the army. I met him when I in-processed him into the duty station. I worked at the Welcome Center in processing new soldiers to the post. As a Personnel Service Specialist (Human Resources), I was responsible for entering personal information into the system and ensuring that the soldier's personnel file was accurate.

Sherman was about nine years older than I was, divorced with three kids, and so ghetto. I was 19 and still wet behind the ears. I let him know about my boo thang in Alaska and our unique situation. Sherman understood, and we started dating.

Dating him started out great. We spent time together laughing, and he taught me so much about army life. We would spend time together on Sunday shining our boots. Not the most romantic thing, but he did most of the shining, and my boots had a high gloss shine on Monday mornings. It made me stand out as a soldier. Sherman and I did other fun things, like going out to dinner, going shopping, watching movies, and taking day trips to other cities. We were having fun.

As time went on with Sherman, he slowly revealed his crazy, deranged side. I was constantly being accused of cheating. I mean daily, and I did not do anything besides work and go back to the barracks.

I remember one time we had to stay after work for a staff meeting. Once the meeting was over, the Platoon Sergeant asked for me and two other soldiers to stay behind, one female and one male. The three of us were labeled as the troublemakers in the company. We were held after so we could receive a stern talking to for 30 minutes. We all left the building together, and as we walked outside, Sherman was sitting in his car right in front of the welcome center. He actually accused us of having a ménage à trois. Unbelievable! I was already in my feelings because I was labeled a troublemaker. Now I had him accusing me of cheating, again. I was really hurt and embarrassed.

During this time, I believed that I could show or prove to a man that I am different from the rest. Make them trust me. I could prove that I am worth it. I tried to prove that I was a good and faithful woman, but Sherman's accusations just got worse. If I did not answer the phone the first time he called, I had someone in my barrack room, and I was cheating. He only became more possessive and controlling.

I was really close to a female soldier named, Landy. She was like a big sister to me. She planned a special girl's night out one weekend. We had not been out in a while, and I was excited, but once Sherman found out about our outing, he completely lost it. In his mind, if I was not making plans with him, I was just wrong. He accused Landy of setting me up with other men. It was horrible, but I still went out.

When Landy and I came back from our girl's night out, Sherman was sitting in the parking lot of my barracks waiting on me. Sherman and I went upstairs to my barracks room, and the arguing began. At first, I refused to back down because I did nothing wrong, and I was tired of him accusing me of things I was not even thinking about doing. However, after a few minutes, I decided to take a shower and went to sleep.

Sherman eventually went to sleep, but he woke up with an attitude. I did not pay him any attention. I figured he would get over it as he usually did, and he did. The next morning things were back to normal or what was considered normal between us.

About a year after Sherman and I started dating, I was honorably discharged from the army after two years of service. The day before I left to come home, Sherman proposed to me. I accepted his proposal, but my heart was torn between Sherman and Ernest. Yes, Ernest was still in the picture. We still talked often, and Sherman knew about Ernest since day one.

Once I moved back to Maryland and was settled back into civilian life, the truth about Ernest came out through a mutual friend. Ernest never intended to leave Alaska, and he was married. Wow! I called him and asked if it was true, and he admitted it. He said we were just too far away, so he settled for someone close. That hurt, but I still had Sherman, and he had proposed. I was more committed to him now than before, but something was not right. It was not right, and I now know what I was doing was wrong.

My desire to marry Sherman came from the hurt from Ernest. Therefore, I continued to tolerate the accusations and arguments with Sherman, because in my mind, I had to get married too, and I had to have a man. Ernest moved on, and so did I.

The same year I was discharged from the army, Sherman received orders to go to drill sergeant school, and he was going to be stationed at another duty station in Georgia. He wanted to get married and for me to move down to Georgia, but something was not sitting right in my spirit about this move. My intuition was telling me do not to do it without securing my own job and money.

I searched for a job and a college I could transfer my credits. I was able to find a school not far from the post he was stationed at, but I could not find a job. Sherman assured me he would take care of me, and I did not need a job, but I felt like that was a way to control me. I am sure he would have taken good care of me financially because he spoiled me with material things. Whatever I wanted, I got, but he was so controlling. I knew if he controlled the money, he would have complete control over me, which scared me to death.

Instead of moving down there, I bought a house here in Maryland near my family. He took a month off and came to visit me, and it was a month from hell. We argued the entire time. I was genuinely unhappy. If we were not fussing because I worked a few hours overtime, we were fussing about who was calling my phone. I was just miserable.

After the month was over, Sherman reported to drill sergeant school. I supported him emotionally through the process. I even flew down to Georgia to attend his graduation. I flew down just for him, but in typical Sherman fashion, I was accused of flying down there to meet with another man. In his mind, I was meeting men while Sherman was at school preparing for graduation. I was baffled. I took time off from work to celebrate this momentous occasion with him. While he was finishing school, I was in the hotel room studying or doing work for one of my classes, but he thought I had a man over. I was so mad that I threw a bottle of wine at his head while in the hotel room. It missed, but that is how mad I was. That was the beginning of the end for us.

We hung in there as a couple for a few months after he finished drill sergeant school, but I was slowly losing interest in him. We finally ended our relationship after almost three years. It happened suddenly. We were on the phone, and again, I was being accused of cheating. Then, it just hit me out of nowhere. You do not have to put up with this. Let it go.

And that is exactly what I did.

I hung up the phone and did not answer it for him anymore. I remember when I told one of my friends it was finally over, her exact words to me were, "I'm glad you ended it because I was scared he was going to hurt or kill you." Now, that blew my mind, but I was glad that tumultuous relationship was over.

LESSONS

Ernest and I were stationed so far away, and neither one of us was putting in the effort to get close to one another. Besides, neither one of us was conducting ourselves as if we were in a relationship. Once everything was said and done, I lost a good friend.

My lesson from Ernest is it is ok to be just friends and that is it. During AIT, Ernest and I had developed a good friendship, which I wish I would have continued instead of advancing into a relationship. I could talk to him about anything, and I was so comfortable around him. Becoming a couple made a difference with us. His dishonesty and disrespect broke my heart. We both said some awful words to one another and have not spoken since. We were like best friends, and our friendship would never be again.

I also learned to love myself and just be me. I do not owe anyone anything. They can take me the way I am or leave me alone. I do not have to prove myself. Take me as I am -- the good, the bad, and the beautiful. I have always liked myself, but the older I get, the more I love myself. Over the years, my tolerance for the drama, the lies, and the bull has become shorter and shorter until I do not tolerate it at all anymore. The only person I have something to prove something to is myself.

I am looking for a provider and protector, a best friend, and a lover in relationships. I am not looking for a father. We should be able to communicate with one another about any and everything. I think it is important to check in with one another to see if the other has plans, but I should not have to ask for permission to live my life. I felt in one of my relationships. I constantly asked for permission to do things like go out with friends or wear a certain outfit or do anything besides breathe and go to work. The jealous and domineering nature of our relationship was extremely unhealthy.

Sherman and I had an extremely toxic relationship. I feared him. He had a temper and would scream and slam doors and throw items at the wall or floor if he felt I was cheating or if I was not doing what he wanted me to do. I honestly thought I could change who he was. This was a complex I developed. I thought I could change people, but people are who they are, and they will only change if they want to change.

Sherman did not see anything wrong with how he acted, which meant he did not want to change. Just like people can take me how I am or leave me, I should have done that with Sherman and just left him because the way he acted and his tantrums were not acceptable.

CHILD'S FATHER

"A time to search and a time to give up, a time to keep and a time to throw away." - Ecclesiastes 3:6, NIV

It had been a few months since Sherman and I broke up for good. A friend of mine invited me out to a party, and I went. That is where I met Rickey. He was seven years older than I, tall, and a heavier set male. He was also divorced with two kids. Never in a million years did I think I would fall so fast and hard for him, but I did.

Rickey was a very smooth-talking gentleman. He took me out on dates, called, and texted me to check up on me in the morning and throughout the day. He seemed like a nice guy. I felt like things had moved so fast between us, but I was happy. In the beginning, he was such a great guy! I remember thinking, how did I get so lucky?

For Christmas that year, which was a few months after we started dating, his ex-wife invited us over for Christmas breakfast. I was shocked! I was not expecting to meet his kids or ex-wife so soon after we started dating. She had remarried and had another child with her husband, and it seemed like Rickey, and his ex-wife had a great relationship for the sake of their two children. We went to Christmas breakfast, and everyone was so nice. His two children adored him, especially his daughter. I thought, wow, this is really a great man, and I loved how the two parents came together for their children on Christmas day.

A few months later, I found out I was pregnant. We were both excited! I thought he was a great dad to the oldest two and a great man to me. He would also be a great dad to our child. We were over the moon excited for this little bundle of joy that was growing inside of me.

About three months into my pregnancy, I stayed home from work. I had horrible morning sickness throughout my entire pregnancy. I noticed that Rickey had not gotten up for work in the past couple of days. He told me he was taking a few days off from work. I did not think anything of it and continued to rest and try to get myself together.

Later that day, Rickey came into my room and told me that he had lost his job because he had missed too many days and had difficulty finding a job because he was a convicted felon. Is this for real? It seemed like something out of a movie. I could not believe this. Here I was pregnant by a man who lied about losing his job and had difficulty getting a job because he was a felon.

Me being optimistic, I told him, "Do not worry. You will find a job, and I will help you, but always be honest with me about what is going on. I cannot help if I do not know." Little did I know that was the first of a plethora of lies to come.

The lying was nonstop with him. I did not know what was a lie and what was the truth. Rickey continued to lie and disrespect me. He went from coming over and visiting me to eventually moving into my house because his cousin had put him out, but he told me he wanted to be closer to me while I was pregnant. He did not pay any bills because he was not working, and when he started working, he was not paying bills because he claimed it all went to child support. Whatever little money he had left over, he would use to go to the club. He did not even hold on to money for gas to get to and from work for the week or to buy himself lunch. He would ask me for gas money, and I would give it to him. I enabled his bad behavior.

Two days before I went into labor, Rickey disappeared for 24 hours. He turned his phone off and did not contact me at all. He claimed he was helping his cousin move, and his phone died, but for 24 hours? That is ridiculous, but I did not fuss with him.

The day I went into labor, Rickey left me in the house alone to take his son to his football game. Once again, Rickey disappeared for hours, and his phone was turned off. My aunt came to sit with me so I would not be alone while I was in labor. My contractions were so intense, and they were coming back-to-back.

My aunt would take me to the hospital, but I was determined to wait on Rickey to return home. I wanted him there with me. He was the father, and I wanted him to be there for the birth of our child.

Once he returned, he was so irritated with me because my aunt was there. It made him look bad for leaving me home alone in labor. I wanted to go to the hospital. He felt they were going to send me home because I was not far enough in labor and kept trying to talk me out of going. I am not sure where he received his medical degree from, but my contractions were coming one right after another, no break in-between. I needed to get to the hospital, and I needed to get there right then! So we went.

Once I arrived at the hospital, I was admitted, and after several hours of labor, our precious baby girl was born a little after midnight the next day. Rickey stayed after I gave birth and left early in the morning. I did not see or hear from him again until the next day when he picked us up to take us home.

I was so in love with my little girl, and I wanted her father in her life. Therefore, I continued to support him and tolerate his lies and disrespect. I knew if I put him out, he would not be involved in her life. So, I put up with the dishonesty, the cheating, the disrespect, and having to take care of him for five years.

About a year after our daughter was born, Rickey was working. He was paying bills. I thought he had changed for the better, but later I found out he was paying bills with bad checks. It took me months to clear up those bills he had not paid and get my accounts back into good standing.

Later that same year, he received a letter from the child support office to support a child. It was not the two he had with his ex-wife. Who is this? He called the child support office and found out it was for a 12-year-old little girl he knew nothing about. He did not believe the child was his, but the DNA test proved him wrong. So now, he had to pay child support for three children.

At the same time of finding out about his third child, the courts were also requesting that he pay restitution for that felony he told me about when I was three months pregnant. Rickey had to hire a lawyer, so that meant he had no money for anything. His lawyer was able to come up with a payment arrangement that satisfied the court. Rickey and I sat down and came up with a budget. He was to pay our daughter's school tuition, and I would cover all the house bills (which I already was doing). That way, he would be able to pay the restitution he owed.

After about three months, he had to report to the court. They received one payment from him. Just one. Where did the money go? He claims he was paying them but could not provide proof of payments. I was furious, to say the least, but I let him stay because once again, I wanted my daughter's father in her life.

We were more like roommates. We slept in separate rooms and coexisted for her only. In May of that year, I emailed Rickey on his work email to remind him to pick something up on his way home. His boss responded, saying Rickey no longer worked there. I called him, and he told me he was playing, but I did not see the joke in it. I ignored him and went on with work that day.

About a week later, Rickey called me and told me that people from the corporate office were there and they were firing people. Then I heard him talking to someone, but I could not hear anyone responding to him.

He told me, "I'll call you back." Five minutes later, he called and told me that he lost his job. They were closing that location and letting the people go. I tried to be positive about the situation. I gave him a pep talk and told him everything would be ok, and we would get through it. Rickey's last paycheck never came from the company, and I thought that was strange. He said he called to check, and they told him it was put in the mail.

One day he was in the basement on the computer. I went into his room looking for something, and there was a letter sitting on his bed from the company that had just let him go. To my surprise, he was let go two whole weeks before he informed me he was let go. I was in disbelief. I could not believe he got up for two weeks and acted as if he was going to work.

Rickey was mendacious, always doing wrong behind my back. He was a pathological liar, and the truth was not in him. So many questions ran through my mind. Why was he lying? Two whole weeks? Where did he go when he was pretending he was at work? What was he going to do now? I was beyond frustrated and annoyed with him.

When I confronted him about the letter, he kept the lie going. He said there was a typo in the letter, but I had already called the number on the letter to confirm the release date, and they confirmed it. He stuck to his lie, and for reasons unknown to me at the time, I let him stay. This was definitely more than just for my daughter's sake because this was extremely unhealthy. It was a toxic situation, and I did not want to be a part of it anymore. I did not want to be responsible for this grown man. He was not my responsibility. Nevertheless, I could not walk away from him.

Rickey had been unemployed now for months, and he was comfortable with it. He had absolutely no income coming in, and he was not providing support for his other three children either, but I was still there supporting him, although he was constantly lying and cheating. If he got a little money from doing an odd job, he would use it to go to the club with it. I honestly think he was going over to another woman's house, but whatever he was doing, he had no business doing it. I knew the relationship was ending when he would go to the club, and I did not care—no fussing or crying. I would tell him to have fun, and I would be at home at peace.

In November of 2009, Rickey proposed to me, and I accepted his proposal. I knew I was starting to get over him, so I do not know why I accepted his marriage proposal at the time. However, now that I look back on it, I accepted his proposal because I wanted the ring. I wanted to be married. I figured, why not marry my daughter's father. I was extremely unhappy, but I did not see me letting him go because I wanted a family.

In the past, he would always ask me to marry him, and I would ignore him or say hell no. However, this one particular day, I said, "Fine, I will marry you," but I was not happy about it, and I do not think he really loved me. He wanted the financial security that marriage brought with it. I did not tell many people I was engaged. Mainly just a few of my friends that I wanted to be at the wedding, but I did not tell my family.

The thought of marrying him bothered me. I would have nightmares about being married to him. God was telling me not to do it, and I knew God had so much more for me in store for me. Rickey could not go where God was taking me.

About a month into the engagement, I called it off. I could not go through with it, but he was still in my house. I prayed to God for strength to let him go for good. A month after I called the engagement off, I finally had the strength to end the entire relationship.

The day the relationship ended, I was at work, and he was at home, not working. One of those "drop you off at work and keep your car all day situations." Instead of dropping me off at work, he dropped me off at my vanpool. I was working an hour away from home at the time, so I rode with a vanpool to save on gas. Yep, that was us. Our daughter was in preschool at a private school. She loved it, so I did not want to move her out of there.

During my lunch break, I started doing my budget and decided I needed to lower some bills. Since Rickey was home not working, he felt he should have the best cable package that was out on the market. That was the first bill that needed to be lowered. I called the cable company to downgrade my package to the basic package. Rickey was furious. He called me at work, and he started fussing. I knew it was over because a calm came over me. I calmly said, "Please be packed and ready to go when you pick me up today and hung up."

That did not sit well with Rickey. He called my cell phone, and I did not answer. He texted me, and I did not respond. He called my work phone, and I did not pick up. So, he started sending me nasty emails to both my work and personal emails. I ignored them all.

That evening when he picked me up, I simply asked if he had his stuff packed. He told me, "Fine, I will leave, but you will never make it without me." I smiled and said, "I can show you better than I can tell you." That night, the lady he ended up having a baby with later that year picked him up from my house. Good riddance to him and hello to peace.

I knew God had me covered, and I praise Him for giving me the strength to let go of him. A month after he left, we had a big snowstorm. About two or three feet of snow fell. How in the world am I going to shovel all this snow? When I looked outside, my front had been shoveled by my neighbor, and the young men in my neighborhood had cleaned my car. Thank you, God, for sending those angels my way.

I knew letting him go would be the best thing for me and my child. It hurt me that what I said about him not being there for her would be true. He was not there for her once he moved out, and it broke my heart to see her in so much emotional pain when he would say he was coming to spend time with her but did not show up, or if she had a dance or piano recital and he didn't support her.

Rickey never updated his address after he moved out, and another child support request came to my house for him. He would not share his current address, which was fine, so I let him know the letter was there. He ignored all the mail that came to my house for him, and a warrant was issued for his arrest for not showing up to a child support hearing.

One morning while getting ready for work, the deputies knocked on my door looking for Rickey. I did not know where he lived. All I had was his phone number. One of the deputies called and informed him that it was best that he turn himself in, and he did that Monday. When he finally did have his day in court, he requested a DNA test, and he found out that he had another child (that is, five children for him). This little boy was about thirteen or fourteen. What was so sad about the situation was that each child he found out about later in life was only a year younger than the two children he had with his ex-wife.

After all this went down, I called his ex-wife to chat. The main topic I wanted to discuss was our children. They are siblings, and no matter what happened with their father, I wanted my daughter to have a relationship with her siblings, and she agreed. She then informed me of the troubled relationship she had with Rickey.

They were childhood sweethearts, and everything he did to me, he did to her. She was the one that informed me that he had recently had another child (he is now up to six children) with the woman that picked him up the night we broke up. I was hurt but was not surprised. I put him out in January that year, and his daughter was born in November that year. He was trying to get back with me after we broke up, and the entire time, he was telling me they were just friends. I guess that was another lie to add to the one million he had already told me. He was extremely friendly with her. So happy I did not fall for him again.

LESSONS

I gained a greater appreciation for life and the small things that most do not care about after this relationship. I walked away from this relationship with the greatest blessing of my life, and that is my daughter. I do not regret this relationship because it changed me in so many ways for the better. My daughter motivates me in ways I never thought of before. I have always been a motivated person, but wanting to give her everything she deserves and raise her right has pushed me to work harder and achieve more than I ever dreamed I could. God has truly blessed me beyond what I could ever imagine.

Once I let go of that toxic relationship, I was at peace. It hurt that he was not as involved in my daughter's life, but the hell he put me through was unhealthy. My child could see I was hurt and unhappy no matter how much I tried to hide it. I wanted him to be involved with our daughter, but he did not want to be. He was always the first person I would call or text if she had an event. There was a slim chance of him showing. I knew I was wasting my time, but I did not care. I wanted him there for her. It was not about him or me. It was about our daughter. I wanted us to be those parents that could be cool for the sake of the child. Now do not get me wrong. The sight of him makes me sick to my stomach, but he is her father, and her having her father is more important.

I would call and tell him, "Hey. You have not seen your daughter in a while. Come spend some time with her, or call your daughter. She has not heard from you in a while." He might call, and that is it. I invited him to every school or extracurricular event, and most of the time, he was a no-show. It broke my heart to see my daughter so upset because he would tell her he was coming and not show or just say he could not make it. As a parent, I have made mistakes, and I overcompensated for the times her father was not there, but she is resilient and understanding. My daughter is my inspiration for a lot that I do.

I finished undergraduate school the year her father and I separated. My five-year-old watched me walk across the stage. I remember her telling me how proud she was of me. I said to myself, "I have a little person watching me, and I cannot settle for anything but the best." I applied to graduate school and was accepted. Around the same time, I was offered a position closer to home, so I did not have to commute an hour each way. Actions are better than words unless those words are used for prayer.

The lesson here is God provides. Moreover, God is able to bless you abundantly so that in all things at all times, having all that you need, you will abound in every good work (2 Corinthians 9:8 NIV). With the help of my family, I was able to complete my Master's in Human Resource Management and was able to grow in my career. My family played a big role in helping me raise my daughter, and I have been blessed with flexible positions at work where I was able to work from home or flex in and out, so I didn't miss an event she had at school and I didn't have to use all my leave either.

I tried to be Rickey's hero. I wanted to save him from himself and from his past and bad decisions. I thought I could mold him into the man I wanted him to be. As a little girl, I always dreamed that I would get married one day, and the man I would marry would be an honorable man, a good man, a wholesome man. Rickey was none of these. However, I was determined to turn Rickey into what I wanted him to be. The man I needed him to be. The father that our daughter required him to be.

Nevertheless, you cannot change a person, especially if they do not want to be changed. Trust me. Rickey did not want to be changed. I believed that if I could change Rickey and he became the man I wanted him to be, I would also be saving Rickey from the destruction of his bad decision-making. I learned you cannot save everyone. You cannot be the hero for everyone. The best you can do is offer advice and pray for them.

Another lesson I learned is to not take it personal or be depressed because people choose to live the way they want. It is their life to live, and I must let them live it. I can either choose to be a part of it or not. I have chosen to walk away from people who bring sadness, depression, negativity, and drama into my life. Right now, I am holding on to peace, happiness, positivity, and love.

In addition, another lesson that I learned from my daughter's father, which had to be taught to me a few times since, is not to hold on for any reason. I chose to stay in a relationship with my daughter's father because I wanted my daughter to have her father in her life, and I did not want to be alone, but I finally had to let it go. His presence in my home and in my life brought me so much misery. I was so happy when I realized it was time to let go. It was hard because I loved him, but it was time. I had held on much longer than I should have, and I was hurting myself. A key lesson I took from this experience was to let go when it is time. One of my favorite sayings is "let go and let God."

MY 30S

"She is clothed with strength and dignity; she can laugh at the days to come." - Proverbs 31:25, NIV

I could not believe it. I had reached 30! Wow, where had the time gone?! I was still doing well working towards my goals, mothering my child, and living life, but I was still lonely. It had been a year since my daughter's father and I separated. During that year, I met a few men, and for most of them, the connection was over after the first conversation or text exchange. Either the men wanted a booty call (sex), were looking for charity, or we just were not compatible.

One day at lunch with my girlfriends, we discussed how difficult it is to find a decent man to date. One of my friends told me she had the perfect guy for me, and she would set me up on a blind date with a gentleman. His name was Willie. He was in his mid-forties. When he first called me, we had such a great conversation. He was divorced with two kids, hard-working, and we both were army veterans. He and I were truly vibing.

After a few phone conversations, he invited me out for coffee. We met at a Starbucks not too far from my house. He shared a few pictures with me via text, but he was cuter in person. Tall, brown-skinned, nice build, and he smelled so good. We ordered coffee, sat, and talked, and that is when things started to change for me.

As he started talking, he explained to me how he was trying to jump-start his rap career. This is new. He did not tell me about this before. He explained how he was living with his mom because all his money was going towards his music career. Now do not get me wrong, I believe you should go after your dreams no matter what the age, but your responsibilities come first. You have to work and have money to take care of yourself and your children and have a place to live.

Then he kept turning his pinky ring and putting it up as he was talking. This was a different man than the one I had been talking to on the phone. His whole demeanor was the total opposite from the guy I was starting to like. I thought I was being Punk'd. This had to be a joke, right? I just knew my friend was setting me up to get on that TV show. I thought Ashton Kutcher would jump out any minute while we were in that coffee shop, but it wasn't a joke. This was the real him. I do not know why my friend thought I should hook up with him. When she said he is a nice guy, I should have been more inquisitive about why she was not dating him. Oh well, you live, and you learn.

He was proud of his life, and his main priority was his rap career. Not his kids or having his own roof place. His life, his choice. I either liked it or would have to leave it alone. I chose to leave him alone. There was no future with this relationship. I wished him well and then moved on.

During another outing with the ladies, I met a young man. He was tall, chocolate, slim and handsome. His name was Lionel. Lionel was a few years younger than I was. He did not have any kids, and he was independent and fun. After a few engaging phone conversations, he and I went on several dates, and I always had a great time with him.

Lionel made me laugh. I felt safe with him, and we would talk on the phone for hours at a time. We were having a good time. My daughter was supposed to go to her father's house every other weekend. When her father did follow the schedule and picked her up for the weekend, I would spend that time with Lionel. He made plans for us to go out and do something different every time. Then one day, he just disappeared after five months into our dating. I had not heard from him in a week. I thought it was strange. What could have happened?

I tried calling him, and his phone went straight to voicemail. About a week or so after Lionel disappeared, he called me. Lionel said he was locked up because of a mistaken identity. I did not believe him. I felt with everything in me that he was lying.

I did my research, and yes, he was lying. He was locked up for robbery. Robbery! Unbelievable. This entire time I had been dating a robber. In all honesty, I was afraid. All types of bad things were going through my mind about what could have happened if he was to rob me or rob someone else while I was in the car with him. I thank God for protecting me.

I cut all communication off with him. I can't do the lies, and being a thief is not acceptable. People work hard for what they have. What gives you the right to steal from them? He was not going to disrupt my peace. I wondered if he had committed other crimes that he did not get caught doing.

A few years later, I researched Lionel's case, and he ended up getting ten years for the robbery charge. After some time, he sent me a letter from jail apologizing for lying and asking if I would wait for him. I was not looking for a pen pal, and I was not willing to wait. Besides, our dating situation ended years ago when he robbed someone and lied about it. The answer was no! I let him know not to contact me anymore and cut off all contact.

After Lionel, I laid low on the dating scene. I was concentrating on my child and myself. One night a girlfriend invited me to her family function, and that is where I met Fred. When I looked at my list, Fred got a checkmark for almost everything. He was single, had no kids, tall, handsome, had his own house, several cars, a legit job, and he was an entrepreneur. From what I could tell, he was honest, and most importantly, he went to church and worshipped God! We hit it off that first night. We sat after the event and talked while my friend and her family cleaned the hall. At the end of the night, we exchanged numbers and started our dating journey.

Fred and I would talk for hours, which seems to be the case with most men when I first meet them. That is because we do not know one another, and in the beginning, there is so much to learn about one another. He made me laugh and loved to travel, which is something I love to do too. We discussed places we had visited and where we wanted to go.

He and I loved the old TV show, Martin, and could sit on the phone and talk about that show forever, laughing and having a good time. The dates were great too! We lived an hour away from one another, but the mini trip down to see him was fun, and we always went to a restaurant or somewhere that wasn't local. It was nice trying new things.

Two months into dating, the phone calls and texts started to come far and few. His "Good morning, beautiful" texts were a daily thing, but that would be the only communication for the day. Things just became strange between us. First, he did not want me going out for Halloween that year. I made plans with my friends months before meeting him and even bought a costume. Fred worked overnight, but he wanted me to stay at his house alone while he was at work instead of going out with my friends. I never understood why. We had plans for me to come down and for us to go out the next day. That night, I texted him that I was leaving the house and told him to have a good night at work, which is when the constant texts from him started.

The first text was requesting me to send him a picture so he could see my costume. I was dressed as a "sexy" firefighter. When he texted me, I was in the car, and I sent him a selfie. He could only see the top of my costume. I figured that was enough. The next text was requesting me to send a full-body picture. I was with my friends laughing and having a good time, not paying any attention to my phone. By the time I looked at it, he had sent me about four or five more texts asking me why I had not sent the picture and if I was ignoring him?

I finally sent him a full-body picture. He was furious once he received the picture. I did not understand why he was so mad. Fred told me I was trying to show out. For who? I thought my costume was nice and tasteful, and I dressed for me, no one else. I asked him what the issue was, and he told me I was running around as if I was single. We were not in a committed relationship, and neither one of us said we were dating exclusively, so I was single.

After his tantrum, I went on and enjoyed my night. I believe the partying ended at 4 am. I really enjoyed myself that night. Instead of a "Good morning, beautiful" text at 8 am, I received a phone call. My phone scared me half to death. I had just gone to sleep a few hours before. It was Fred. Who else would it be?

I answered my phone, and he was literally walking out of work. "So I see you made it home. Are you alone?"

Fred was so dramatic. I said, "If you are done with the dramatics, I will get myself together and come down there for our date," and I did just that. Once down there, Fred acted standoffish towards me like he was in his feelings. Am I not supposed to go out? I tried talking to him, but he was pouting, and that is so unattractive to me. I went home after dinner.

A few weeks after Halloween, Fred and some of his friends were going out of town. We talked that day before he left. I told him to have a good time, be safe, and we would talk once he got back. I figured if I showed him respect and trust while he was away, he would do the same for me when it was my turn to travel. I sure was wrong. Fred did not even show me trust while he was in town. Why would he do it when he was away?

He wasn't texting or calling as much when he was home, but when he was away, he was sending me random texts, and if I didn't respond quickly, there were several texts inquiring what took me so long to respond. He wanted to know what I was doing and who I was with.

As usual, I pray for signs to stay or go, and they were clearly right in my face, but as usual, I thought he would change once he saw how awesome I was. This was not true. In usual fashion, three months of dating and the real person came out. The third month of dating Fred happened to be my birth month, December. I had planned a trip earlier that year to go to Aruba with my friend Darlene whose birthday is in the same month as mine.

I was expecting Fred to show me the trust and respect that I showed him when he traveled, but that is not what happened. He and I spoke the night before the trip. He was on his way to work. Before we got off the phone, he asked me to call him once I was settled at the airport. I told him sure and said goodnight.

The next morning I picked Darlene up from home, and I drove us to the airport. As I was getting on the shuttle, I heard my phone ringing, but I could not answer it because, as usual, I was overpacked and trying to get my suitcases onto the shuttle. Once I was settled on the shuttle, I looked at my phone. There was a missed call, voice message, and text from Fred. I did not listen to the voicemail until I was settled at the airport.

To sum up the voice message, Fred chastised me for not calling at soon as I made it to the airport. He told me to have fun, but not so much fun that I slept with someone else. After I got my thoughts together, I called him back and asked him why he left such an ignorant message. He replied by asking why I hadn't called him.

After a few minutes of back and forth, I finally decided to end the call. It was my vacation, and I did not want to deal with it. There were random texts from Fred throughout my trip. The daily good morning text was one of them, along with the same annoying meddling questions.

Once I returned from Aruba, things between Fred and I were extremely strange. I should have let go, but I wanted it to work because, honestly, I was tired of being alone. So I continued to date him. Fred and I had decided not to date exclusively. We did not talk often, but when we did, our conversations did not involve much talking. We would sit on the phone listening to one another breathe. We did not really text either. It was a very peculiar situation.

After the New Year, Fred and some of his friends went to New Orleans for a long weekend vacation. The Friday of his trip, I had to work and was extremely busy. I was not paying any attention to my personal cell phone. Once I was done for the day, I had several missed texts from Fred. I was thinking, Lord, why does he act like this?. I refused to get into another argument with him, and that is when I knew this was the end of this situationship.

Once settled at home, Fred called me, and I was at work. It was late on a Monday, and everyone was mostly gone from the office. I closed my office door and broke off our situation. I told him things just were not right, and I was tired of being accused of cheating when we were not dating exclusively or even a couple. Fred said he knew this was coming, and that was it. That was the end of our dating journey.

I have seen him once since we dated and we spoke to one another. We have no hard feelings or animosity toward one another. We both are adults and realized it was not meant to be for us.

A few years after the Fred dating experience, I met Lawrence. One day at work, I was sitting in the cafeteria talking to two coworkers. Lawrence approached the table to speak to one of my coworkers. That coworker excused himself from the table and left with Lawrence. Once they left, my other coworker and I went back to our desks.

Later that day, I was sitting at my desk when the coworker from earlier that day who excused himself to talk to Lawrence came to my desk and asked to use the phone. I thought that was strange, but I let him use it. He called Lawrence and handed me the phone. Lawrence and I talked a little over the work phone. He asked for my personal number so we could talk, and I gave it to him. He called me that night.

Lawrence and I talked for an hour that night and had a good conversation. He was different from other men I dated. Lawrence had two side businesses. He turned his passions into income. Lawrence's full-time job was where I worked, and he worked in the IT department. He was very intelligent, self-taught in his profession, and a passionate man. I really admired him. He did not have any children. He had an apartment near the full-time job, and he owned a house in Pennsylvania.

Dating Lawrence was fun. We went out almost every other weekend, and no matter what we did, we had a great time. He loved to spoil me. Whatever I wanted, I got. I did not ask for much, but he always surprised me with things. He was so thoughtful. I was not used to being spoiled like he spoiled me. I am the independent type. I always felt like I did not need a man to do anything for me. Lawrence was different. He did not care about any of that. He was a provider, and he loved to buy things for me.

We worked different work schedules, so the only day we were in the office together was Thursdays. We usually had lunch together depending on our schedules that day. When we first started dating, he let me know that one of his side businesses really picks up during the summer months, so we would not see each other as much. My love language is quality time, so I knew that not spending time together would be hard for me, but I said l would try it. Besides, I really admired a hardworking man.

Before summer officially started, Lawrence's side business picked up. He was on the move. He was booked, overbooked, and rebooked. He traveled out of state a few times. I was happy for him, and he was exhilarated doing what he loved.

As the summer went on, we would go weeks without seeing each other. He would leave work early on Thursdays, which meant we did not even have lunch together. Memorial Day weekend, he worked his side hustle the entire weekend and was off on Memorial Day. I packed a picnic lunch and went to his apartment. I laid a blanket out on the floor as if we were in the park, and we ate and enjoyed ourselves.

By the time the end of July came around, we only saw each other on Thursdays if then, and if we did see one another, that was only for a quick lunch break because he was usually taking leave so he could prepare for the side job he had to do that night. I still did not say anything. I just went with the flow because I wanted to be supportive, and he did warn me about his summer schedule when we first met.

After months of briefly seeing each other, Lawrence had a weekend off with nothing scheduled for either side job. He told me he wanted to spend the weekend with me. I was excited. We made plans, and I looked forward to it. That Friday was supposed to start our weekend together in a long time, but my daughter's father canceled picking her up, so I had to develop other plans.

My mom could keep her, but not until Saturday, so our Friday outing was canceled. He understood and told me he could not wait to see me the next day. The next morning I woke up, dropped my daughter off, and texted him to let him know when he was ready. I was packed and ready. Lawrence was a night owl, so he usually slept late, and I did not want to disturb his rest that morning. He texted me about an hour later, and I left out for our time together. Well, the time I thought we would have together.

That morning he woke up to someone requesting his services. He could have ignored them because he is his own boss, but he did not. So, as usual, I got a few hours Saturday and a few hours Sunday while preparing for the jobs he accepted.

I was extremely upset about our special weekend being ruined. I was tired of being put on the backburner. I understood he had to work, but what is the saying? You make time for what you really want. I was starting to see he did not want to spend time with me. It was frustrating and hurtful. We decided to meet up at a neutral location to talk.

I expressed my anger with the situation and told him how I felt. I demanded more time. Lawrence assured me he would try to do better. We hugged and parted ways. A week after our discussion, Lawrence broke it off with me. I could tell he was not happy after we talked the week before. He told me that his side businesses came first, and it was not fair to me. He needed to be alone and continue to work hard to build his brand. I was hurt, but I respected his decision and let go. Of course, there was more to it than he just needed to be alone.

A few months after we broke up, Facebook suggested a friend to me. I went to school with the woman, and her profile picture was of her and Lawrence at a Christmas party. I went to her Facebook page to look at her pictures. I read a post she posted in November that read, "I usually don't post pics of me and my beaus, but I am in love this time." Wow!

I wondered how long they were dating for her to be in love. He broke up with me in September to work so he could focus on building his business. Is this the side business he was putting all his energy into? I was heartbroken.

I texted him, shared a screenshot of his girlfriend's profile picture, called him everything but a child of God, and blocked him. A year later, I ran into him and his new girlfriend at the airport. I was going to Jamaica for my birthday, and they were going too. I was past the pain and anger. I smiled, spoke to him, and kept it moving. We were on the same flight, but thank God we were not at the same resort.

LESSONS

During this time, the biggest lesson I learned was to pay attention to the signs God is sending you. God sent me signs in each situation, and I ignored them or asked for a clearer sign. I do not know if I needed a big sign that said "no" or "stop" to fall from the sky and land in front of me, but clear signs of trouble were there. Indications to walk away or let it go. In conclusion, the signs were there, and they were clear. I just needed to look, listen and pay attention to them.

Lawrence was the one who taught me how to receive. I know it sounds crazy, but I am not a good receiver. I am a giver. I am a doer. I make it happen. Like many single moms, we are going to get it done. However, I always say I want a protector and a provider. Well, how can he provide for me if I will not accept or ask for it? He taught me that. I have learned how to accept and say thank you. I do appreciate him for that lesson.

Mindfulness is another lesson I learned while dating Lawrence. I have been told before that my mouth was a weapon and my words cut like a knife, and I would speak without thinking. I had no filter. If it came to my mind, it came right out of my mouth without a second thought. Some people thought of me as a mean person, but honestly, I never thought I was. I would always say I was just candid.

Lawrence is the first guy I have dated that sat me down and talked to me about my hurtful words. He helped me to see that you can be honest without being so harsh. He also helped me to see that not everything requires my input. After our talk, I reached out to my psychotherapist, and we worked together on me being more mindful. Being mindful was not just watching what I say but also about slowing down to examine the situation and think. I learned to ask myself questions before I react. What is going through my mind? Why do I feel this way? Is this issue mine or theirs? I have let go of a lot of anger and aggression through this process. I also improved my communication skills.

I always thought I was a good communicator. I took pride in my great communication skills, but in reality, I was just screaming a lot of hateful and mean words and not really communicating how I felt or what the issue really was. Over time while working with my psychotherapist, my communication style changed. I walked away from this relationship with great life lessons that have helped me become a calmer and better person.

I also learned if the person wants to, they would. If he wanted to spend time with me, he would have figured a way to do so. If he wants to talk to me, he would call. Stop accepting the bare minimum or nothing at all. I learned to stop being put on the back burner. If you do not have time, let it go completely. I learned to stop holding on, hoping things would get better. As I said earlier, the signs were clearly there. I just needed to be more observant and obedient.

LADDER

The Narcissist by R.H Sin: "Let's be honest, most of the guys I've mentioned have a narcissistic nature, but this guy, in particular, is the sickest of them all. He says he loves you but treats you like he hates you. He claims to miss you but rarely shows up. He says sorry but never intends to change his actions. This guy would rather see you in pain. This guy is the reason you're reading this now."

When I read that poem on narcissism, I said that explained this next gentleman so well. I have heard of a narcissist and even dated a few, but this guy was very different from the rest. After having the experience of dating him, I will never forget. Ladder was a combination of all lessons before, present and future, that I needed to learn, and the lessons were taught at the advanced expert level. Time spent with him was really a challenge in itself.

I met him online when my friends and I decided to try online dating. There were some nice guys and some weirdos, but there was one guy that caught my eye. His legal name was Ernest, but his nickname was Ladder because of his height. He was 6'7. Once we matched, I started exchanging messages daily on the dating site. I wanted to talk on the phone with him, but I was determined not to ask for his number. He was going to be the one to do all the asking.

About a week or so of us messaging on the dating app, he finally asked, "How does this work?"

"What do you mean?"

"Could I have your phone number?"
"Sure!" I gave him my number, and he called me immediately.

We talked on the phone for two or three hours that first day. I happened to be off from work, and he works outside of the office, so we were able to talk without any interruptions. After a short break to attend to our children that evening, we continued our conversation later that night, talking and laughing on Skype until we both fell asleep. We were acting just like teenagers in love. It was so cute.

He asked me what kind of man I was looking for. To sum it up, I told him I was looking for a Godly man that is independent and secure in himself.

A man who would treat me like a queen and did not have "baby momma drama." A man who loves to travel and can communicate.

I asked him what kind of woman he was looking for. Ladder told me he wanted an independent woman that did not have "baby daddy drama." He also mentioned that he didn't want a woman that acted "ghetto." We discussed our past, future, and present situations.

The next day after talking on the phone for hours, we made plans to meet in person. I did not have much time because I had to go to a program at my daughter's school, so we met in the parking lot of a shopping center near my daughter's school. He was even more handsome in person. Tall, medium brown skin, dressed nice, and smelled so good. He hugged me so tight. It felt as if we had known each other forever. We did not want to part ways, but I had to go so I could get to my daughter's school for the program. Before we parted ways, we made plans to go out on a date that weekend.

I left our meeting on cloud nine. I felt as if he was the perfect gentleman, and he had a majority of the characteristics I was looking for in a man. There were some flaws, but we are all flawed. No one is perfect, but he was a Godly man, a family man, a true gentleman, tall, handsome, had a nice build, clean, a hard worker, and had his own. At least, that is what he led me to believe in the beginning.

We continued to talk on the phone and went out on dates regularly. Every Sunday, he would spend quality time with me from the time he dropped his son off at work until it was time to pick him up. We were a month in, and I was still digging us. We were not anything serious, but it was getting there. I really enjoyed myself whenever Ernest took me out. It was my time away from reality. He treated me so special, like a queen. When I was with him, he would tell me my hands did not touch my purse, a door, or a gate. He would open the doors, and he even opened the gate leading into my yard for me. A true gentleman. Oh, and how he made me laugh. I would laugh until my stomach hurt. We were truly having a good time together.

One Sunday, about a month and a half after we started dating, I had plans to go to brunch with the ladies. These plans were made well before I met Ladder. My girlfriends are busy professionals with children and/or husbands. We have to plan our outings far in advance to ensure we can all make it. This was our time, and I always look forward to meeting up with my ladies for a good time.

Ladder told me to have fun and said he wanted to stop by to see me after brunch, which was cool. He then called me back and said his daughter called. She wanted to spend time with him, so he could not make it until later in the evening, but he would make it up to me. I told him not to worry about it. Our kids always come first. I loved how he was spending time with his kids. So we made plans for later that evening. I was actually happy about that change. I knew my girlfriends and I always took our time. We sat, talked, and laughed so I did not have to rush or worry about meeting him at a certain time. It all worked out perfectly.

About two hours after our phone call ended, I left out to meet the ladies for brunch. As I was parking, I received a text from Ladder saying, 'Hey, what are you doing?" I ignored it because we had already discussed our plans for the day, and he was supposed to be spending time with his daughter. I joined my friends for brunch, and I had a great time.

When I got home, I had a slight headache, so I took some Tylenol, washed my face, wrapped my hair, and put on my lounging clothes. As soon as I sat on the bed, my phone started to ring. Who else would it be besides Ladder?

When I answered the phone, he immediately began screaming at me. I was confused and was not quite sure what the issue was. I told him to calm down and explain what the problem was. He stated that I was out forever with whoever, and it probably was a man. At this point, my head was pounding. I calmly said, "I told you where I was going and with whom. Besides, I thought you were spending the afternoon with your daughter."

"Well, her mom wanted her home to do her hair, so we did not get that much time together."

"Ladder, I do not know if you are upset because of the time being cut short with your daughter or if something else is bothering you, but you will not take your frustrations out on me. I am going to take a nap," I said right before hanging up.

I fell asleep, and I do not know how long I was asleep before my phone started ringing. It was Ladder, again. I answered, and he apologized for his actions and asked me to call him when I woke up. Once I woke up, I called him, and things were back to normal. That was the first sign of the real Ladder.

A week had passed since the Sunday Brunch incident, and I asked Ladder to be my accountability partner for a 10-day green smoothie fast I was going to do. I told him the date I planned on starting and my entire plan for it. He suggested I start the next day. I said no because I had to plan it right if I wanted to be successful. Ladder said, "Well, I do not want to talk to you until you start," and hung up on me.

I was furious. Who in the hell did he think he was talking to? Did he think this was helping me, or is that what I needed from an accountability partner? He even had the nerve to text me to ask if I changed my mind yet. I told him I did not need his help and not to contact me anymore. He called me back, asking why I was being so dramatic. I explained his actions were not acceptable and I would not tolerate the disrespect. Once again, he apologized, and things went back to normal.

Later that month, my coworker invited me to her house warming, and I took Ladder as my date. We had such a great time at the party. When we left the party, we returned to my house and sat in the living room talking and laughing. My daughter was at a skating party, and her father was picking her up.

My daughter decided she did not want to leave the party once her father arrived, so she was ignoring him, and he called me whining about it. I told him he is her father and he needed to put his foot down. What did he want me to do? I was not there.

When I hung up the phone, I laughed because he was such a punk when it came to his daughter. I always joked with him about how his daughters had him wrapped around their little fingers. Ladder took total offense and started screaming at me. "That is not funny! Why are you laughing at him?"

This was a Ladder I did not know or like. He actually scared me. The real Ladder was slowly coming out. He could not hide the real him for much longer. You would think that would have been enough to make me walk away from him, but I did not. I stayed around. I was hoping that man he was in the beginning would come back, but that is not who he really was.

Ladder was a very controlling and emotionally abusive person, and he only got worse the longer we stayed together. That man he pretended to be in the beginning never came back. At this point, the real Ladder was completely unhidden, and things only got worse.

The day before Mother's Day, my car broke down about 10 minutes away from my father's house. I called my dad to come and give me a jump, and he did. Once I got home, I called AAA to replace my battery because I thought that was the problem. Then I called Ladder and told him what had happened. He told me, very angrily, that he should have been my first call. I explained to him my father was closer, and I felt it made more sense to call him. We went back and forth until I finally agreed with him.

My car ended up needing more than a battery, and it was towed to the mechanic for a new alternator had to be put in it. I picked up my car on Monday and was good to go. The following Friday, I had a nail appointment. When I arrived in the parking lot of the nail salon, my car shut off. (Sidenote: Can we talk about how good God is. Thank you, God, for allowing me to make it safely to my destination and parking before my car cut off. I digress.) Per Ladder's request, he was my first call. He told me to call AAA to have the car towed, and he would pick me up and take me where I needed to go once I was done at my appointment.

I was off on this particular day, and he was working. I called him after my appointment, and he came right over to pick me up. He was on the other side of town, but he wanted to do it, and I really appreciated him for that. It turns out it was actually my battery this time. By the time he picked me up, my car was ready for pick up. When Ladder arrived, he had an attitude and kept it the entire time I was in his car. He told me not everybody gets to do "nothing on Friday."

I was confused because picking me up was his idea. I had other options: Uber, Lyft, my sister, phone a friend. It really would have been ok if he did not come and pick me up, but he did. He dropped me off to pick up my car and told me to call him once I was home.

Father's Day that year, Ladder and I talked on the phone that morning, and the day was going great. He had stopped spending Sundays with me, so I did not see him that day. About an hour after we got off the phone, he called me back and was extremely upset.

About a week before, I had blocked him on Instagram. I know it was childish and petty, but we had got into an argument, and I wanted it to end, so I blocked him on everything. I forgot I had blocked him until he called me that day. He was so upset. He cussed me out, hung up, and blocked me. I was distraught and so hurt that I cried that night. That should have been the end, but it was not. We did not talk for three days. Then, unexpectedly, he sent me a text saying, "I love you. Why do you continue to hurt me?" and I fell for the foolery. I let him right back in, and he was my date to my father's wedding reception that Friday.

I knew it was a mistake allowing him to be my date to my father's wedding reception for so many reasons, and when he complained about the wedding reception being on a Friday and how people had to work, I should have told him never mind and went alone. Instead, I ignored his complaints and told him I would meet him there. When he first arrived, he was the sweetest. He hugged me so tight. He went to the buffet to get us some appetizers and brought them back to the table we were sitting.

We were talking and laughing, and then it was as if a switch flicked on in him. He changed completely. I did not know what was going on. He was being dismissive and being just plain rude. I tried talking to him, and he said this is not the place, but I did not understand what happened. I was so upset. I asked him to dance, and he told me no. I told him since he was so unhappy that he should leave, and he did.

My sister could see how disrespectful and mean he was. She was concerned because it was as if he did not like me. I felt like it was payback for something I did in the past. I was a very different person in my youth. I was unkind, and I could be disrespectful at times. At this point, I believed he and I had met in the past, and I gave him a hard time or was mean to him. I asked him what I could have done to make him treat me like this. In the end, I realized it was all him and his issues. It had nothing to do with me.

For the first three months, Ladder tried his best to hide the real him. The spiteful, rude, controlling, insecure person was hidden initially, but as time went on, the real him slowly creeped out—the evil person, the one that took joy in seeing me cry and unhappy. After a while, the only thing that was consistent about him was his "Good morning, beautiful" text and him being mean, jealous, and unsupportive. Those things never changed, but the dates and quality time stopped. The phone calls went from daily to weekly to none. It was horrible, and I was miserable, but I continued to make excuses for him.

In July of that year, I went to the Essence Festival in New Orleans. I had booked this trip a year before, and Darlene and I were going. I was so excited because I always wanted to go to Essence, and I needed a break. Ladder came over the night before to stay with me. Usually, when Ladder stayed the night, he would be gone by 4 am so he could go to work, but this particular time he stayed until about 7 am. I thought it was strange, but he stayed just to start drama between him and me.

When I woke up, Ladder was laying in the bed staring at the ceiling, saying he could not believe I was leaving him. I ignored him and asked if he was going to be late for work. He said he was taking his time, as he was depressed. He slowly got up, got dressed, and left. I went about my day getting ready to leave that night—the usual routine of hair, nails, and last-minute packing.

Once Darlene and I arrived at the airport, I received a dramatic text message from him saying his transmission went out in his car and his world was falling apart because I was leaving. I asked Darlene how to deal with him. Darlene does not have tolerance for foolishness, and she is the realist of my friends. Her response was, "Block him." We know I did not.

I stayed in New Orleans for four nights. The entire time I was there, we had not talked on the phone, but we did share a few texts, mostly of him accusing me of cheating. I did not give his texts a second thought. I read them and kept moving. I enjoyed my trip. Darlene and I had so much fun. I ate good food and the concerts that weekend were everything!

On my last day in New Orleans, I woke up to a text from him asking if I was at the airport yet. No good morning, how are you or anything. I am not sure why it made a difference if I was at home or not because he did not spend time with me. I responded and let him know I was not at the airport because I had a late flight and that I would text him once I was settled.

When things started to change between us, I tried to communicate with him about how I felt. Remember, after my last relationship, I worked with my psychotherapist to improve my communication skills and be more mindful. I calmly tried to talk to Ladder about how I was feeling, how things had changed and how I felt towards the changes and us not spending quality time together. Immediately he became defensive. He would cut me off, tell me it was all in my head and that I just like to argue.

I let him know I do not like to argue, and he continued with his dismissive ways. Because of his unwillingness to communicate, I stopped trying to talk to him, and I just accepted the bare minimum he gave me.

The relationship was on and off for several months. I would get tired of being mistreated and ignored, so I would cut him off. He would always come back with sad eyes and sweet words, and I would accept him back. I remember telling myself, "I am too old for this ish," but I did not permanently walk away.

Darlene told me when I was finally fed up, I would walk away for good. I honestly wished he was really that man he pretended to be in the beginning -- the sweet, loving, and kind man -- but he was not. That man would never come back again because he was not real.

We were on and off most of the time, but we were on in December, my birthday month. He came over the night before my birthday to spend the night. Nothing had changed, and we had not been out on a date since May (if you do not include my father's wedding reception). He was still controlling and mean, but I was so happy to have him there that night. He bought me a nice gift, two tubes of Rhianna's lip-gloss (which I needed more of) and pink Calla lilies. They are my favorite flower, and pink is my favorite color. The night was great.

The next day, my birthday, my friends and I were going to Virginia to see Martin Lawrence's Lite AF Tour. I was super excited because I am a huge Martin fan. Three of my closest friends and I were doing a girls' trip. I was elated.

That morning he woke up and did not wish me a happy birthday. He just started the day off with an instant attitude. I asked him what was wrong. His response was, "You aren't dumb figure it out." I asked was it because I was going away? He said he did not care about that. I was so irritated because he refused to talk to me, and he would not tell me what was wrong. I was extremely annoyed, and I did not know what else to do but cry. I was so hurt. As soon as I started crying, he got up and said, "Guess it is time for me to go."

Now I have cried around him several times, usually out of frustration or because he had said something hurtful for me. He never comforted me, ever, and I thought that was strange, but this time I saw the joy in his face once I started crying. That is when I realized he took joy in my pain. He never said, "I am sorry, baby. Here is the issue." He got dressed and said, "I will talk to you when you return." I was upset, but I went to VA with my girls and had a great time. He texted me once and told me he loved me, and I ignored the text, and I did not hear from him anymore while I was away.

I returned home the next day, and I had not heard from Ladder in over 24 hours. He liked the pictures I posted on Instagram (I had unblocked him, and we were following each other), but I didn't get any texts or phone calls. After I was settled at home, I reached out to him. Why? I do not know, but that was the start of another intense argument.

Once again, I am not sure what happened. I just know he was screaming, and this time I was screaming right back at him. I hung up on him and started texting my good girlfriends to give me that "sister girl, do not let him get to you" talk. They calmed me down, but I sat and wondered. Why do I end up with similar types of men? I seemed to attract the same type of man and end up in an unhealthy relationship. This particular relationship was extremely toxic. The situation with Ladder had to be the worst I had ever experienced.

I prayed, talked to my mother, and listened to my girlfriends. After some serious self-reflection, it hit me suddenly. Just stop and reflect on yourself. I needed to take time out from dating. Build a stronger, more intimate relationship with God. Work on healing my issues and fears. I needed to slow down and take my time with this process. What God has for me is for me, and His timing is always perfect. That is when I called it quits. I told Ladder I was done, and this time it was for good. Finally, I let go.

LESSONS

"Anyone can treat you right for a short period of time, but it takes a special person to treat you well over and over again, for the rest of your life." - Vex King. December 19, 2019

The first lesson is to stop making excuses for bad behavior. I am famous for doing that, and I made an excuse after excuse for Ladder's behavior. He had a bad day at work, or he was reassigned at work, or something broke in his house, and he has to get it fixed, or he is stressed. None of that is a reason to be disrespected, ignored, or treated badly—none of it. Life happens to us all, and we all must find ways to deal with it. There is no reason to take your frustrations out on someone else. Also, if there is a problem, communicate like adults do not throw a tantrum like a toddler.

The next lesson is to let go completely! I did not completely let go. I would occasionally communicate with him via text, and there were a few times I let him come over to stay the night. Whenever he was around, I had anxiety, and when he left, I was angry. Not only was I angry with him because of something he said or did, but I was angry with myself for allowing him and his toxic ways to come over to visit.

Each and every time he came to my house, he had something negative to say about me or my house, my job, you name it, but I still would give in every few months or so and allow him to come over. He was so toxic and so miserable. I knew we would never be a couple, but I would not let go completely. I wanted male companionship. I liked being held and having someone to talk to. I guess I had to learn the hard way, and I did.

It got to the point that whenever I let him come over, something would go wrong the next day, either at work or at the house. First, it was the toilet. Then it was a small leak followed by my furnace until I missed something major at work (which I rarely did). I believe there were all signs to let Ladder go. I had to cut off all communications and contact with him.

Some people cannot go where God is taking you. He was a blessing blocker. For me to move on to the next level, I had to let him go completely. This was an issue with a few other relationships. Once I let go for good, I was elevated to that next level, or I got that job I had been waiting for a while. Something I have been working on or praying for happened. My blessings were released.

Another lesson learned that seemed to apply to my life period was to slow down! I always seemed to be in a rush, and I do not know why. I have learned that God's timing is always perfect, and if it is for me, it will not pass me. That goes for my dating life too. My husband will find me when the time is right and not a minute before.

I rush into relationships before knowing who the real person is. Tyler Perry's famous character Madea says you need to see a person in all four seasons, which is true. You need to see them when they are mad, sad, stressed, and happy. In addition, wait to see who they really are. In the beginning, everyone is sweet and lovable, and I realized that with most of my relationships, I fell hard and fast for the person he pretended to be when we first met. I wanted to be in love so bad that I fell for the wolf in sheep's clothing just about every time.

I also need to pay attention. I am a talker, and I will talk a person to death. I need to shut up, listen and be more observant of people. I also learned not to tell so much when I first meet and definitely not tell them what I am looking for in a man. When asked, just say I will know when I see it. I stopped telling them because he will pretend to be what you are looking for, and he will seem like Mr. Right. The entire time he would be acting, and I would fall in love with the person he pretended to be. Let the man be who he is going to be. He is either the right one or not. Either way, it is ok to walk away.

Also, reflecting on my relationship with him, I realized me being so independent and successful was a big issue for him. I would minimize my success just to make him feel bigger. I would not respond to him when he would talk very disrespectfully to me. I dimmed my light so he could shine, and I did it out of fear. He never hurt me physically, but mentally and emotionally, he was harsh.

Now, do not get me wrong. I do not brag or try to make people feel bad about what they might not have. I am very humble, and I know everything I have was given to me by God. I like to share my accomplishments with my significant other. I would believe he would be happy for me. That was not the case with Ladder; he would always downplay my accomplishments and make me feel like I had not accomplished anything or there was nothing special about it. The fact that I did not ask him for anything and I was able to do great things for my child and myself made him angry. I did not understand where it came from and why it was there, but I do realize it is his issue, not mine. My dating journey with Ladder taught me it is ok to be humble but know my worth.

There is a difference between being arrogant and being proud. It is okay to be proud of your accomplishments and to share your successes with people—especially when dating someone. You should encourage and motivate one another, not be scared of sharing your success or failures.

EPIPHANY

"For God is not a God of disorder but of peace- as in all the congregations of the Lord's people." - 1 Corinthians 14:33, NIV

After Ladder and I finally broke it off, I was lonely, so I attempted online dating again. I am not sure why I tried it again, but I did. A co-worker and I both decided to sign up for a different online dating site simultaneously. The site I tried was similar to the one I was on when I met Ladder. Several weirdos and couples were looking to become a thurple.

A few guys that I matched with I quickly unmatched with after we exchanged a few messages. Some were looking for just sex, others were looking for a sugar mama, and some were just not compatible. After a month of matching and unmatching with men, I met two guys that I was kind of feeling, and we eventually exchanged numbers.

The first guy I exchanged numbers with was Chauncey. Chauncey was two years younger, tall, dark, and street smart. He was a slimmer build. Smaller than I am used to, but he was charming and funny. He did not have any kids, and for the most part, he was independent.

During our first phone conversation, he was honest with me about his criminal past. He shared with me he did time in jail when he was younger for a nonviolent crime, and he learned his lesson and had no intentions of going back to jail. He was a hard worker, smart and kind. I could tell from talking to him that he had learned his lesson and grown from his time in jail.

After a few phone conversations, he invited me out on a date. We met at a restaurant, of my choice, for dinner. He looked just like his picture, so no catfishing was there. Chauncey and I had a great time eating and talking. I do not think I laughed that hard in a long time, and as you know, I love to laugh, but something was not right. It felt as if something was missing. I am not sure what it was. I tried to shake the feeling, but it would not go away.

Although I enjoyed myself during the first date, that weird feeling stopped me from going on another date with him. Therefore, I did not make myself available for a second date. Then I was not available to talk. Something was not sitting right in my soul while dating him. Eventually, I let him know I did not want to date him and left him alone.

The second guy I met on the dating site was Keenan. He was tall, muscular, light-skinned, handsome, and smelled so good. He was well educated, divorced with one daughter. I found our conversations to be intriguing. Different from Chancery's, but I enjoyed conversing with both.

Keenan and I went on two dates. On the first date, we met for a quick lunch break. He was working from home, and I was off from work. We met up at a restaurant close to his house and ate. It was a nice date. The food was good, and the conversation was better. He asked if we could go out again one day soon and next time after work hours so we could have more time. I said sure. A few days later, we met up for dinner. This date did not go as well. The conversation was not as intriguing as usual, and it was just something not right about him. Once again, something was not sitting right in my soul. At the end of the date, Keenan hugged me and said he could not wait to take me out again. I was thinking to myself, slim chance that was going to happen. After the second date, I let Kennan know I did not want to date him any longer.

I met two great guys who made me laugh and were different in their own ways, but I still was not feeling them. I could not figure out why I did not really want to go on another date or continue talking to either of them. Then it hit me. It is not them; it is me. I do not need to date right now. I could not believe those words came out of my mouth. I was feeling indifferent about dating. I was ok being alone, enjoying my own company, and I was truly happy. I had peace.

My loneliness caused me to enter into some unhealthy and toxic situationships, but now I come to appreciate my alone time, and I have enjoyed it for some time. Appreciating me and being fine with being alone is important. It helped me to get to the point where no one or nothing could interrupt my peace. No matter how, fine, sweet or kind. If they come to disrupt my peace, they have to go, but it was not just about disrupting my peace. It was also me taking time for myself.

I took time out to focus on myself, and I was happy and relaxed. For the first time since I can remember, I was not concerned about meeting a new man or going on a date. I changed my total mindset when it came to dating and my life. At this point, I was committed to bettering my life for my daughter and myself. Dating had moved so far down my to-do list that it was actually towards the end. This was my time to shine, and I wanted to resolve was my anger, unpleasant attitude, and negative thinking. Healing was at the top of my list.

HEALING

"Forgive yourself for all the times you made a choice in ignorance! You didn't know." - Jerry Flowers

Through the years, I have met and dated some interesting people. All came with their own set of lessons and blessings. Even if it was someone I met and talked to for a short period, I learned something from the experience. The last dating experience was so intense and harsh that it caused me to take a step back from dating and think about life. I had put an overdue pause on my dating life, and I was exhilarated about it.

After I had my epiphany moment about putting the brakes on dating for a while, I did some deep reflecting and thinking. I sat with my feelings from my last relationship. The hurt, the pain, the disgust, the lies, all the bad and the ugly of that relationship. Then I processed my feelings. I cried, screamed, journaled, prayed, and talked with my psychotherapist. Whatever it took to process the feelings from that relationship so I could let go and move on.

Once I finished processing my feelings, I thought, what should I do next? I quickly realized that healing was at the top of my checklist during my dating hiatus. I knew that I needed to focus on myself, and I did just that. I took my time with the healing process, and I dug deep because I wanted to heal entirely, mind, body, and soul. If I did not take the time to heal, I would continue to repeat the same life mistakes and attract the same type of hurtful relationships. This process to me was about healing myself completely, not just so I would stop attracting the same types of men, but so I can be a better mother, daughter, sister, and friend. A better well-rounded person. More Christ-like.

I have always understood what was meant by the saying, "hurt people hurt people," but I never realized how much that statement was reflective of me. When I was hurt or angry, I would try to hurt others by using harsh words or calling them mean names. I would scream and holler profanities. Be as disrespectful and mean as I could be. To me, I wanted my words to cut deep. My tantrums when I was mad were horrible. I also realized that some of the men I dated were hurt, either from past relationships, their childhood, or a combination of both. They were hurt, and I was hurt, and although most hid their true identities in the beginning, there were signs. Signs of how bitter they were when I would listen to them describe an ex-girlfriend or something that happened in their childhood. I am sure people could tell the same with me. How hurt I was from my past relationships. The pain I held onto from my childhood. I had not realized until I started my healing process that I still held onto childhood pain.

Healing was long overdue for me. I prayed and worked with my psychotherapist to let go of my pain—all of it. I was honest with myself about what, who, how, and why I was hurting. It was a long process but so worth it. Letting go of the hurt meant I had to forgive. So I worked on forgiveness. Forgiveness is not just to the men I have dated but to my family and friends who have hurt me. I wrote detailed letters to all who have hurt me, and I put all of my feelings in those letters. I put all my anger, rage, sadness, frustrations, annoyance, and all feelings on the pages of those letters. It felt so good to get all that rage out.

I believe I wrote thirteen letters. I really addressed all of my pain areas and went deep. I prayed and let the pen flow. When I finished writing, the letters I did not mail them to the individuals they were addressed to. Instead, I read each one then burned them. I did not mail them for two reasons. Either I am not in touch with them anymore, or I do not know where they live or because I felt bringing up these old issues would cause even more issues now. For me burning the letters was my way of releasing the pain for good. This process helped me to release my anger and forgive the person whether they are sorry or not.

The forgiveness part was for me, not them. I needed to heal and move past all of the negativity that I had being hold on to for so long. I had been holding on to some pain for thirty-plus years. Angry with people who did not know and honestly probably did not care that I was angry. People that were enjoying their lives, and I despised them for one reason or another. Holding on to hate and anger is madness. Holding on to that anger was giving me anxiety, and a few times, it made me physically sick. Letting go, forgiving, and leaving the past in the past felt like a weight was lifted off my shoulder. I happily "let go and let God." Now, I do not hold on to anger anymore. I may have my say at the moment about the situation, but I do not keep talking about it. I let go and move on.

As far as the men I have dated, I would tell myself things like, "Oh, I can fix him," or "Once he sees how great I am, he will come around." This was never the case because I am not a fixer, healer, psychologist, or any other intervention these men needed to heal. They did not believe anything was wrong with them; therefore, healing and change were impossible because if they did not see what was wrong, how could they see what to fix. Three I had my own issues I needed to work through. I needed to heal, I saw my issues, and I was ready to continue to dig deep, expose them, sit in my pain, acknowledge it and work past it.

Instead of focusing on others' broken pieces, I focused on my own. I did some self-reflecting on my own issues. Why was I so accepting of toxic, disrespectful, self-serving relationships? What deep issues did I need to work on? Why was I scared to be alone? I prayed, journaled, and talked with my psychotherapist, and I realized that I had a complex about being alone. I never quite discovered where this complex came from, but I felt like I had to have a man, a piece of a man, someone that I could say was mine. Through this process, I have found that there is a blessing in being single. It is ok to be alone and not to accept anything else besides God's best for me.

I also could not figure out why I was so quick to get mad and react without thinking. Through my healing process, I have learned to calm down, I developed thick skin, and I stopped taking things so personal. I remember a coworker from years ago having framed q-tips on her desk. I thought it was strange so I asked her. "Why do you have q-tips framed on your desk?" She told me it was a reminder to quit taking it personally (Q-TIP). Interesting, but I really did not take heed to the phrase until I started my healing phase. Now it is a big part of my daily life. I realized that most of the time, the issues people have with me are not with me, but their issues, and I apply Q-TIP when dealing with them.

Applying Q-TIP to my life truly helped with my anger. I was an angry woman. I also realized that I had to find my own happiness and stop looking to others for it. My happiness is my responsibility. I took this time to evaluate my likes and dislikes. What made me smile and spent time with myself. I prayed for peace and guidance. I learned how to go out and do things alone. If I wanted to go out to eat, I went solo, and I was comfortable with it. If there was a movie I wanted to see, I would go see it alone. During this process, I mastered being alone and being comfortable with it. When the right one comes along, I will adjust to his presence, but I am content with being solo until then.

Next, I reflected on my self-esteem, and I always thought that I had high self-esteem, but if I did, I wouldn't allow misery and disrespect in my life, so I started working on building my self-esteem, and my happiness started to shine bright. I realized that I alone am enough and that when I am ready to date again, he will add to my life, not be my life.

My attitude will not depend on him and how he treats me. I have never been the type to be unhappy if I was not in a relationship, but I would complain occasionally to my girlfriends about being tired of being alone and wanting a man. Yes, I get tired of having to do it all when it comes to my home, car, and life in general, and some companionship would be nice too, but I rather do it alone and be happy, rather than being in the wrong relationship and miserable.

Most of the men I was dating were not helping me in those areas, so I was miserable and still doing it all on my own. That is just lunacy. I am giving all praises to God for blessing me with all I need and the ability to do what needs to be done. I pray that He continues to give me the strength to do it until He sees fit for me to have a mate. It will all work out for His good.

Self-respect is one of the keys to a peaceful life. How could you demand respect from someone else when you do not respect yourself? Self-respect has always been important to me. I was raised to have respect for myself and to carry myself like a lady. Dress like a lady, hold my head up and do not allow anyone to be disrespectful towards me with their actions or words. Yet, I was allowing myself to be disrespected by the men in my life. I allowed myself to be disrespected, treated like an option. I even hid my success just so a man would stay around. During my healing time, I realized that permitting all this to happen was me disrespecting myself. No more! Now I know and see the wrong in my ways. I have corrected it, and I will not allow it to happen again.

Discernment is the ability to tell the good from evil, and it is something that I have but ignored. I would get that urging feeling to leave someone alone. Walk away for good, and I would ignore it. Sometimes the feeling would be telling me to run. Run fast, and I would still ignore it. Trusting myself and using my discernment is something I realized I was not doing. I could sense the evil and cold-hearted ways of others, but I doubted myself and continued to be around them and allow them to interrupt my peace.

During this process, I realized that discernment was there. The signs were always loud and clear, but I ignored them because I felt I needed a man. I also believed what others told me I was being too hard on people and not giving them a chance. All along, it was not me being so hard on people. It was my discernment kicking in, and it was telling me not to trust this one. Listening to others, I ignored the bad vibes I got from others and allowed them to stay in my life. Then I would always ask God for a sign. Should I stay or go? All while the signs were right there, and I was choosing to ignore them. Healing helped me to start trusting myself more and using discernment when dealing with others in all situations. I now see my discernment as a blessing.

Growing up, I was taught to be you. Be proud of your uniqueness and never change who you are for anyone. To always be me. I found it important that I never lose myself for anyone, but I have done just that several times. I am a good person, and just like everyone else, I have flaws.

In my 20s, I was more comfortable with being me, and I would always say, take me as I am or leave, but for some reason, in my 30s, I would adjust to make the man happy. I would modify by not talking as much or not speaking my truth about something, holding back my real feelings. I would change how I communicated just so he would be happy, but I was dying inside. I was miserable but was being quiet about it to make him happy.

Another difference between my 20s and 30s was, I would argue. My communication was harsh, but in my 30s, I learned how to effectively communicate my thoughts and feelings after working with my psychotherapist. Still, I just wouldn't express my feelings to the men I was dating just to keep the peace. For the most part, they did not know how to communicate. They believed that when I was trying to communicate about the issues, I tried to start an argument, so I just kept quiet.

When I sat down and started my healing process, I realized that I was altering me and my communication style to make the man happy, and I was so miserable. It all goes back to me believing I need a man.

Another reason I pretended to be someone different was out of fear. Not the fear of losing him, but the fear of physical or emotional harm. A few of the men I dated would act demented if I stood up for myself or cracked a joke or if I was just being me. So I pretended to be someone else. No more of the acting! I am unapologetically me.

Now I communicate, but I also am picky about whom and how I will communicate. I found that some people are not worth the energy of long communication. I will say what I need to say and then let it go. For others who are worth the time and energy for me to voice my concerns, cares, hurts, pains or love, I take my time to talk and explain my point. I have become a great active listener, and I do not scream harsh words anymore. Actually, I do not scream anymore, period. I am more mindful about what I say and how I say it, but I say it. A calm has come over me. I have peace, and I am going to protect my peace. I will not change myself to make anyone happy. I love my uniqueness, my characteristics. I just love me.

UN-FOOLISH

"The way of fools seems right to them, but the wise listen to advice." - Proverbs 12:15, NIV
"Healed people hear differently." - Unknown

I have always been an independent woman. In my 20s, I believed I could help a man become a better person or, in some cases, become a man, but like the singer, K Michelle said, "you can't raise a man." Looking back now, I laugh. I thought I could mold some of the men I dated into the men I wanted them to be. He was who he was, and I could not change that.

I remember reading a quote that said something like a woman cannot change a man, but a man will change for a woman he wants. After my different dating experiences, I see just how true that statement is, and in some cases, the men are not going to change because they are who they are. If I took the time to slow down, I would have seen what type of people they were. I would have seen through the ones that were smooth talkers. I could have seen that we were not compatible and did not want the same things in life or in a relationship. I would have also seen the envious and hateful behavior, but instead, I ignored it, and I believed I could change them.

In some cases, I thought I could change them, but most of the time, I stayed even though I saw there was no changing them. I was hoping they would be the men I was trying to change them into. They would see I was worth the change and actual change. Some of them actually pretended to be what I wanted them to be for a little while, but that fairytale did not last long. I was waiting on them to be the men I fell in love with. Now I realize my peace is so much more valuable to me than dealing with the drama and craziness. I deserve a genuinely good man of God.

It was my belief whenever I met that I could mold him into what I wanted him to be. Until he was the man of my dreams, I would put up with just about anything. I honestly believed if I tolerated the disrespect, lies, and foolishness, it would pay off because he would soon be transformed into the man of my dreams. That is just foolishness. Once I matured and realized a man was who he was, and the only one that could change him was him.

I was still tolerating foolishness, but different types of foolishness this time around. At first, I dated men who wanted either women they could control or wanted a sponsor. After those relationships, I realized I am not to be controlled, and it is not my responsibility to ensure that a man is taken care of. I have a big heart, and when I was younger, I was very naïve. I would fall for a sob story or feel bad and felt it was my duty to provide and make sure he had. I now realize he was not even trying to do for himself. This was a game, a hustle for him. Oh no, honey, you will not hustle me. My kindness will not be taken for weakness anymore.

Another practice I have stopped is providing wife benefits to a boyfriend I cut off, allowing him to live in my house, driving my car, cooking, cleaning, and washing his clothes. I made sure he had gas money to get to work and lunch money. I was more like a mother than a wife, and I sure was doing more than a girlfriend should be doing.

I have a big heart. I care, and in the past, my big heart had been taken advantage of. No more. I was used for what I could offer or the benefits they received from being my "boyfriend." What did I receive in return? Being used, lied to, cheated on, and mistreated. The disrespect had to end, and it had to start with me respecting myself enough to walk away from anyone or anything that was not giving me the respect I deserved. In addition, I have learned to do just that. My "peace out" game is strong!

I could not see it at the time, but I gave so much love, time, energy, money, and myself, and I was not receiving any reciprocity. I would give until I could not give. I could not figure out why I was so tired and depressed. It was because I was giving my all to someone and was not receiving anything in return. When I didn't want to or have it to give, they didn't leave. Instead, they would cheat with women who would give them what I would not give them and kept holding on to me. I believe they were trying to break me. They stayed around because I allowed them to. Now that I learned to walk away, my mind is clearer, I have more energy, and I am not depressed. It is weird how people around you can affect your mind, body, and soul. I am now more conscious about who I let into my space, friend, family, or others.

I would lie to my friends and family about my relationships with men because, in my mind, they had to seem great to everyone else! In all honesty, my relationship was none of their business, but at the same time, I should not have to lie about my beau's activities or the way he treats me. I am sure my real friends and close family members could see through the façade. No relationship is perfect, and there will be ups and downs, but my peace will not allow me to stay in a relationship that has more downs than ups.

As I matured, I stopped dealing with men that were looking for financial support, and once I healed from past dating experience, I did start to attract financially stable men. I dated some nice men that spoiled me financially, but something was not right with these men. They were emotionally and mentally unstable.

I am not sure if these men were traumatized from something from their childhood, a bad breakup, or a combination of both. It was an emotional rollercoaster dealing with insecurities and emotional instability. They thought they could throw money at the situation to make it better. Now I am once again dealing with inconsistency, lies, and mental games, but I did not stay around long. I had learned that my peace was much more important. So, I would leave.

Three months was about the length of the honeymoon phase with the mentally unstable relationships. Ninety days is how long they could hide the real them. The insecure man, the mentally disturbed man, and once we reached that quarter year point and his true colors started to show that is usually when I was out. My growth was impressive.

I had grown so much, and this is how I knew. When I cut the men off, it was not a bad breakup, yelling and throwing things. I would not block his number and never wanted to see him again. It was calm communication and letting them know this is not working and that is over, but we are cool and speak if we see each other's type of separation. I then pray for them and release any pain or anger I may have. I only put three months into dating, so I was not so attached. I have learned to take it slow and get to know the person. A person can only suppress their true self for so long.

Growth has truly come from my several different dating experiences, and I learned a plethora of lessons. The most important of the lessons is realizing that the change had to start with me. That I had to stop accepting less than what I deserved, and I had to first, and most importantly, respect myself—trusting my intuition and walking away from toxic and miserable people immediately instead of holding on to see if they will change.

There is so much happiness in my world. Why choose to be unhappy and used? I will not participate in foolish behavior anymore. Blessings and happiness are flowing freely in my life. With prayer and hard work, I have effectively set boundaries and raised my standards.

JOY

"Thank you, Next." - Ariana Grande

I am extremely grateful for my lessons and experiences I have encountered over the years. Some lessons had to be taught a few times, and each time the lessons were different, some more intense than before. Some left me broken-hearted and denying that real love exists. I have focused on my healing and I took time to heal wholly.

My time healing was for me. This book is the last part of my healing process. While reflecting on my past hurt, I also decided to reflect on all the joy that has been brought into my life over the years. I am immensely grateful for all the blessings in my life that have brought me so much joy.

My relationship with God would be at the top of my joy list. I was not raised by parents who went to church weekly, but we always knew about God. My mom joined the church when I was in high school, but I did not join the church until I was older. I joined my mom's church, a great church, but it is a mega church, and I realized I prefer a smaller, more intimate church, and I found one. I would go on and off, but I eventually started going weekly and getting more involved in the church by joining a ministry and volunteering for events. I also watch another church weekly online. They are located about an hour away from me, so instead of traveling, I listen online after I get home from my home church services. I also participate with their corporate church fast and other virtual church functions they offer. I read my Bible daily, and I pray and talk with God. I now look to Him for guidance first. Sometimes I ask family and friends, but God is always first on my list. I am thankful to God for all He has done and will continue to do in my life.

Next on my list would be my daughter. God never makes mistakes, and He truly did not when he blessed me with her. As I stated in my previous chapter, she inspires me to put the most effort into all that I do. I have taught her a lot as her mom, but she has taught me so much more as my daughter.

One of the most important things she has taught me is how to love unconditionally. My daughter has taught me patience, forgiveness, and how to play more and stress less. Through her actions, she encourages me to strive for my dreams and never give up. She was only five years old when I finished my bachelor's degree, but I remember how proud she was of me. The day I graduated, she hugged me so tight and said, "You did good, Mommy." Her smile and ambitions bring so much joy into my life. I am truly grateful for that little girl.

My family brings me joy. They are not perfect by far, but they have always been there for me. My family has always supported me with my goals and aspirations. When I went back to school to get my master's degree, my family supported me by helping me with my daughter. She was taken care of on the nights I had to go to class, and she kept her overnight when I had a lot of schoolwork or just needed a break. I could never thank my family enough for all the love and encouragement they have given me over the years.

As the oldest sibling, I always felt my parents and other family members were harder on me than on my siblings, and I used to be angry about it. I couldn't understand why my family was so strict with me and lenient with my siblings, and I still don't know, but I recognize it was all that helped to get me to where I am today. I am strong, independent, and blessed! I look back now, and I am appreciative of the tough love that was given.

Through it all, I have grown so much, and I have no regrets. I have so much joy in my life. All events in my life helped me to grow in so many ways as a woman of God. Pastor Battle of Zion Church in Landover, MD preached a message one Sunday titled "Perfect Mess." To sum the message up, he said that God will put you in the perfect mess to bring you closer to Him. You cannot always play the victim. You must accept your role in the process, take the pain, and learn.

I am not a victim in any of these situations. Sometimes I gave hell more than I received it, and in some situations, I received hell when I was trying to give peace. Either way, I learned, and I am thankful for the lessons. God snatched me out of my repetitive toxic dating cycle, and I had to sit in pain for a while, process, and move on in order to heal, learn the lessons, and receive the blessings that were meant for me. After I processed the pain, I found that joy was all around me. Joy was within me. I am joyful.

"May the God of hope fill you with all joy and peace as you trust in him, so that you may overflow with hope by the power of the Holy Spirit." - Romans 15:13, NIV

PURPOSE

"For we are God's handiwork, created in Christ Jesus to do good works, which God prepared in advance for us to do." - Ephesians 2:10, NIV

Recognizing and reflecting on my dating lessons has been an amazing process. I put in the work and did a lot of self-healing, self-love and released a lot of pain and anger. I had a few ah-ha moments and realized just how blessed I truly am. This process was truly rewarding to me.

Next, I reflected on discovering my purpose. I always felt I had a calling to help people, but I did not know how. I have a Master's in Human Resources. When I enrolled in graduate school, my passion was to work in Human Resources (HR), but after working as an HR liaison for a few years, I felt like there was something else I was called to do.

My next thought was to become a psychologist, so I applied to graduate school to get another degree in psychology, but after thinking and praying about it, I decided not to go back to college. I felt being a psychologist was not my purpose. I also did not feel like going back to college, and I surely was not going to take a placement test (GRE or GMAT) to go back to graduate school. I was on a search to find my assignment from God.

After a year or so of searching, I had not figured out what my purpose was, but I still felt a calling on my life. I had researched several different options, but I was not comfortable with them. I prayed about it, asking God to reveal my purpose to me. I was not sure what to do or how to figure it out. Then one Sunday, one of my friends was leaving the country for a teaching position. Before he left, he invited his close friends to join him at his church and brunch. That is when I started to get back involved with church.

Before this, I would show up every now and then. I always paid my tithes electronically, but I would never get involved. But after going with my friend that Sunday, I started going to my home church every Sunday. I also got involved in church by joining the education and training ministry.

One Sunday, while attending my home church, the pastor preached a sermon about finding your God-given gifts so you can give back. The pastor suggested a survey to help figure out what your God-given gifts were. My top two results from the survey were administrative and teaching others.

After completing the survey, I was still unsure of what my assignment was. I continued to pray and research. Initially, I thought since I love to travel and always planned trips when my friends and I traveled, I was supposed to be a travel agent. I was super excited! I thought I had found my purpose. Immediately I started researching how to start a travel agency. I found a host agency, which I thought was a great fit for me.

The agency was designed to help startup travel agencies, and being a new travel agent, it was just right for me. A host agency offers great tools, training, and booking platforms and helps with marketing and other important business tools. I would be an independent contractor, and I paid a yearly fee and a percentage of my commission to use the host agency resources. The host agency offered well-established booking engines and a lot of excellent training. All of this was important to me, a newbie in the travel industry.

Once I successfully finished my initial training that was required to join the host agency, I paid my annual cost to join. Next, I came up with a name for my travel agency, set up a website, and started to market my business. Everything was up and running, and then COVID-19 hit, and the world shut down, travel came to almost a complete halt, and the travel industry took a devastating hit.

I was upset. How could this happen? I finally found my purpose, and now this. I was baffled, but it gave me time to pray and think. I talked to God and asked if being a travel agent was my true calling. That is when I realized that I love to travel and only plan for me and my friends when we travel, and honestly, I prefer a travel agent myself to handle the details of big trips. Truthfully, I did not want to plan travel for others. It was not where my passion really was. Eight months after opening my travel agency, I shut it down. I was not sad but rather appreciative I had the experience, and I learned a lot from the short time I operated the travel agency.

When I was closing my travel agency, my full-time job offered career development training, and I signed up for a few classes. A few days before one of the trainings, the instructor sent an email to attendees with some directions and other information for the training. I noticed next to her signature were the initials ACC. I was curious about it, so I Googled it, and on the International Coaching Federation (ICF) website, I found it, Accredited Certified Coach (ACC). I had to find out more. What is a Coach? Do they help others? If so, how? How can I become a coach? I was filled with excitement and enthusiasm! Have I found my life purpose? Will this be my way of giving back?

I did extensive research on the coaching field, and I was sold. I prayed for reassurance that I found my assignment, and I received it. Yes, this is it. Was I passionate about coaching? Yes, I was! In coaching, you provide support, accountability and help draw the answers out of the client. Usually, when a person discovers their next step or solution independently, they are more likely to respond and act on it than if they are told to do something.

There are no certifications or education requirements to become a coach, but I wanted to learn more about coaching, and I felt if I had the training, I could offer my clients the best service possible and be a great coach, continuously perfecting my gift. I decided to take the training required to pursue my ACC certifications, and that is when my search for the perfect training program started.

The ICF website listed certified programs that offer the required training hours to become ACC certified. I found a few I liked and looked more into them. Life Purpose Institute (LPI) was one of the first programs I researched, and they offered a free introductory class, so I signed up for it.

The training was conducted by the founder of the institute, Fern, and listening to her talk, I knew LPI was the place for me. Fern started her career out many years ago as a psychologist (one of the first fields I initially looked into), and after many years, she felt she wanted to do more for her clients, and that is when she decided to become a coach and eventually opened her own coaching institute. I felt connected to Fern's story. No, it was not mine, but I felt a connection, so I signed up for the ACC path to coaching program with her institute.

Training and certification are not required to become a life coach. I chose to take trainings and pursue certifications to offer my clients the best service. I want to show up and give my clients the best coaching sessions so they can get the results they desire or more than they ever expected. I wanted to be prepared and have different techniques to handle any situation.

Training has helped me to become a better coach. I have learned different methods of coaching, and I can provide my clients with excellent coaching services. As of this date, I have completed all three courses I need to take before I can apply to become ACC certified. I am a Certified Life Coach (CLC) and enjoy what I do. My niche is helping successful women work on their mindset, discover their purpose, and set and achieve goals. I eventually want to launch a program to help young women work on their mindset to help prepare for adult life. How cool is that!

I went from searching for my life purpose to helping other women find theirs. Through trial, era, and prayer, I discovered my purpose.

I am passionate about helping other women who know they have an assignment but are unsure what it is. I have a zest for coaching. I find it exciting, and I truly enjoy working and helping others. Thankful that I found my purpose.

BELIEVING FOR GREATER

"Now to him who is able to do immeasurably more than all we ask or imagine, according to his power that is at work within us."
- Ephesians 3: 20, NIV

"Lord, by such things people live' and my spirit finds life in them too. "You restored me to health and let me live." Surely it was for my benefit that I suffered such anguish. "In your love you kept me from the pit of destruction; you have put all my sins behind your back." - Isaiah 38:16-18, NIV

Discovering my gift and sharing it by walking in my purpose has been so exciting and rewarding. In the past, my focus was always on a boy or man. At one point in my life, I was more focused on being in a relationship than anything else. I wanted to live my life my way. I did not listen to others, and I was not listening to God.

True, I went to college and received my degrees, but it is in what I was interested in at the time. I do not regret getting my degrees in the major I was interested in at the time of applying. It was a great learning experience for me. I believe all that has happened in my life has helped me to grow into a better person. It has made me well-rounded, knowledgeable about several subjects. I am stronger, independent, and a more understanding person.

I never really knew there was a life purpose until I was older, and I certainly did not know my purpose. I am happy with my full-time job, and being a mom is my most important and rewarding job, but I felt like something was missing, and that was coaching. My coaching business is an exciting and fulfilling side business that I plan on building and making full-time by the time I retire from my full-time job. Prayerfully I can retire early. Being able to help others discover their life purpose or coaching them through other difficult parts of their lives has been incredibly fulfilling.

My lessons from dating, along with other life experiences, have helped make me a better woman. These experiences have also led me to find my life purpose. They have also helped prepare me for my purpose partner. I believe my purpose partner will be the man that will balance me out. What he does not do well, I do, and what I do not do well, he does.

I desire to be provided for and protected, and through the process, I realized my actions have said differently. I have done the deep healing and figured out what my underlying issues were. I learned how to be happy alone. I no longer feel I have to have a man, and I am not settling for just anyone just to fill that urge. It is better to be alone than to be miserable with someone that is mistreating me. My happiness depends on me and no one else. Now I will not allow any disruption to my peace. I have come to realize that it is ok to walk away if the situation is damaging my joy and peace.

I am grateful for the lessons I have learned and the blessings that have come from them. My focus now is to continue being a good mom to my daughter and continue building my coaching business. I know God knows my heart, and His timing is always perfect. If I would have met my purpose partner before I healed. I would not have known how to love him properly or what our partnership purpose was. I would have hurt him, been disrespectful, and I would not have appreciated him. When God sees fit, He will send me my purpose partner. Until then, I have peace and joy, and I will continue to walk in my purpose. I am deserving of God's best.

I will continue to trust God and build my coaching business, helping other women discover their purpose and passion. Throughout life, I have been on my own path, doing my own thing. Now I look to God to guide my life. He has put me on the path of life coaching, and on this path, I have met several people who have helped me shape my coaching skills and build my business.

I am thankful for my past, and I have no regrets. Lessons learned. In addition to learning lessons, I am sure I was a lesson to some. All was needed to bring me to where I am today. God can and will do more in my life than I could ever imagine.

KARLA L. MCCULLUM 109

I am looking forward to the blessings God has in store for my life and my business. I am praying for continued growth in all areas of my life. I am excited about the growth in my business and helping other women discover their purpose and passion. All I have experienced has helped me grow and get me to where I am today. I am exceedingly thankful for it all. Thank God for all blessings. I am looking towards the future and believing in God for greater.

"Blessed is she who has believed that the Lord would fulfill his promises to her." - Luke 1:45, NIV

Made in United States
North Haven, CT
01 November 2021